THE PURPOSE BASED RETIREMENT

Forget the Silver Bullet

Straight Talk for Your Golden Years

By Casey Weade

Dedication

I would like to dedicate this book to my grandparents. I would not be where I am today without their wisdom and encouragement. Never underestimate the impact you will have as a grandparent. Never take for granted the blessings you will receive as a grandchild.

Howard (1925-2004) & Christine Weade (1928-2013)
Ralph (Born 1927) & Myrna Bailey (Born 1940)
Lauretta Bailey (1930-1991)

Proverbs 17:6 "Children's children are the crown of old men; and the glory of children are their fathers."

Howard & Christine Weade

Ralph & Loretta Bailey

Ron & Diann Weade

Table of Contents

Foreword

Begin each day as if it were on purpose. ~ *Mary Anne Radmacher*

When I'm asked to speak to a group, I sometimes start with a game of what I call "verbal flash cards." Regardless of the topic, I ask the audience to give me a one-word definition of what the topic means to them. I'm always amazed at how diverse the responses are – even when you would expect universal agreement.

In the classroom, a teacher would hold up a large card, for example, with a picture of a horse. The class said "horse" in unison, and the word was written on the back of the card. Sometimes the teacher held the card with the word showing instead of the picture. Students would verbalize the mental picture sparked by the letters, h-o-r-s-e.

Allow me to flash the word "retirement" at you, dear reader. What mental picture does your mind paint? How do you define retirement? If you look up the word, "retirement" in the Merriam-Webster dictionary, it says: *"withdrawal from one's position or occupation or from active working life."* I don't know about you, but when I read the word "withdrawal," I think of moving back from something, retreating. When armies fail, they retreat. It sounds negative to me.

When I flash the word "retirement" at my seminars and ask for a one-word response, I never hear the word "withdrawal." What I *do* hear are words like:

> Golf
> Beach
> Grandchildren
> Freedom
> Fun

Occasionally, a few serious-minded folks in the group who have already connected the dots and know we're there to talk about money will offer words like:

Investments
Income
Money
Medicare

In one audience, a man in the back row blurted out, "Strangle my broker." Everyone laughed. I decided not to tell him he was two words over the limit.

After conducting hundreds, if not thousands, of meetings with pre-retirees and retirees over my professional career, I found one common misconception. Many people believe retirement is **all** about money and investing. Even if you don't believe that to be true, there must be some reason why you are spending time reading this book, when you could be out playing golf or tennis, fishing, or enjoying your grandkids. Probably, the answer lies in the fact that you, like almost everyone else, are concerned about your financial security.

Retirement should be a time to finally do what you wish with your life. Instead, some people are fraught with anxiety over what's happening with their financial affairs. This is true even with some who are wealthy. There is always the concern wealth, and the security it provides, may vanish overnight. If you don't believe that, ask some of the folks who lost a sizable chunk of their life savings in the last stock market crash because of poor planning. Or interview someone who labored under the delusion that property values could never decrease and sunk all of their assets into real estate prior to the bursting of the last housing bubble.

A truly happy and financially secure retirement means you're confident about the future. It means your brow is not furrowed with doubt and anxiety about what Wall Street is doing. It means you do not feel compelled to stay glued to CNBC to see what the talking heads say about the trends of the market. It means that you do not feel obligated to hover near your computer, watching the scrolling ticker on your account screen. In short, it means you have peace of mind.

In my tour of duty on the retirement front lines, I've come to the conclusion that retirement, in the sense that you leave the work force, is not for everyone. Some people I know love their work so much that, to them, work is recreation. One man, for example, owns three automobile dealerships. Although he has plenty of capable employees in place to watch his businesses, he still loves to hang around the showroom floor. He says he loves the atmosphere of the place. To him, relaxation is looking through the automobile section of the classified ads. He knows how to play golf, but he would much rather look for a good deal than he would a golf ball.

My father retired when he was in his early 50s. He planned to relax, spend quality time with family, and, most importantly, he said, he planned to play some "serious golf." That lasted a year. Ron Weade was the kind of man who loved the game of golf, but the game just didn't love him back. He contracted a case of what golfers call "the yips." If you ask him, he'll tell you "the yips" is a debilitating golf disease that makes it nearly impossible for you to make a putt of any length. Even "gimmees" of three or four feet can't find their way into the cup. So, within a year, Dad was back at work. Not because he needed the money, but because he felt a certain sense of fulfillment in helping clients that he couldn't find on the golf course. Many of these individuals were people with whom he developed friendships over the decades he spent as a financial professional. The irony of it all is that after he returned to the workplace, he lost "the yips." He actually enjoys the game more, now that the golf gods have restored his putting stroke to where it was before − average.

Seriously, there is a dynamic at work there − an element of the human psyche that psychologists probably have a term for − that makes it impossible for some people to relax when relaxation is all they have to focus on. My father and I get along very well, but when he was suffering from "the yips," I actually had to quit playing golf with him because it was too painful to watch. On one occasion − no joke − I saw him miss a three-inch putt. To his credit, however, at no time during his bout with this strange golf disorder did he wrap his putter around a tree, heave his golf bag into the water, or cry. But he did decide golf didn't give him the sense of accomplishment he needed out of life. My father was always what you would call a "driven man," in that he was determined to succeed at any endeavor, overcoming all obstacles in his way.

This obstacle, however, was different. During his one-year retirement, he discovered something about himself. To be happy, he needed to do something. He needed to set goals and achieve them. He craved the challenge of the business world. So, after his one-year hiatus, he set out to establish and build a new financial practice. As I write this, my father is 63 years old and still working and loving every minute of it. From time to time, in casual conversation, he will wistfully mention retiring, but I can't picture it. I doubt he will ever be able to give up the career that brings him true happiness and personal fulfillment.

Perhaps it runs in the family. My grandfather, Ralph Bailey, still works at the ripe old age of 85…not out of necessity, but because he is doing what he has always loved. His field of endeavor has always been education. He became a school principal at age 25 and was a leader in the field of education in Indiana. For him, education was not so much about the accumulation of knowledge as it was the development of character. My Grandfather Ralph is all about honesty and integrity. To him, passing along what you've learned to others who need to know it is simply part of the human obligation, which is why my focus as a financial professional is, to this day, more about education than it is about numbers, and more about people than it is portfolios.

When you're contemplating what retirement means to you, think about your dreams and your goals. Are you at that stage of your life where, when asked your age, you begin thinking you should make some life decisions? Are you receiving offers in the mail to join retirement organizations? Are you perhaps surprised to find that you qualify for discounts here and there that weren't available to you a decade ago? Anyone refer to you as a "senior citizen" lately? Did you look around wondering to whom they could possibly be referring, because it certainly couldn't be you? Do you find yourself absentmindedly thumbing through brochures on retirement? You know the ones – happy, smiling people with healthy shocks of salt-and-pepper hair, strolling on the beaches, holding hands, or sailing, or playing Frisbee with what could only be their grandchildren. Do you ever get the feeling that maybe you're at a crossroads, or at least a fork in the road, where you need to make important "pathway" decisions? When it comes to your financial future, are your goals crystal clear, or do you need a little Windex on that pane of glass?

One expression that always irritated my grandfather was: "He who can, does; he who cannot, teaches."

"It's just not true," he protested. "Teachers – good teachers, anyway – don't do what they do because they **failed** at something. They are driven to share what they know to improve the lives of others."

He's right. I've played golf with many golf coaches who are great at the game. They can stroke the ball with absolute grace and near perfection. Their drives are straight and their putting is true, and their fairway game is deliberate and sure. Many of them learned by practice and intense concentration how to play the game and play it well. Some turned professional and were successful, but later decided the schedule of a touring golf pro was simply too demanding. I know excellent golfers who teach the game but have never had an interest in turning professional. Who knows how famous some of these folks could have been? But it just wasn't what was important to them. But what the best golf instructors I've met seem to all have in common is a gift for teaching. They understand the nuances of the swing, the physics of the game, the interaction between the ball and the club face, the aerodynamics involved with the flight of the ball – everything about the game. They not only understand it, they can **articulate** and **demonstrate** it, thus enabling them to share what they know with others. They have the unique ability to help you develop the physical and mental characteristics that will allow you to become better at the game. That is their passion and their gift, and it shows.

A competent financial coach is one who possesses both the technical know-how and the ability to communicate that knowledge to clients in such a way that each client will be able to (a) crystallize his or her goals and dreams for the future and (b) understand what is required to achieve them. It will be a different walk for each client. Why? Because we're all different. We have different dreams, goals, visions of the future. Just like those "verbal flash cards," our responses may not be the same as those of our neighbor when it comes to retirement and what it means for us.

In the game of golf, not all coaches are alike. Some specialize on the short game. Some specialize on the long game. Some specialize in the physical aspects of the game and some concentrate on the mental aspects. For those nearing retirement, a specialist is required, as well. To continue with the golf analogy, you're now playing the back nine. The traps are unique and the water hazards are of different configurations than what you may have experienced earlier. Choosing the right financial advisor is a critical decision that affects your peace of mind and could ultimately lead to a worry-free retirement.

I don't care what the dictionary says; these are not the days to withdraw. These are the days to move forward to the most exciting time of your life. They don't call them the golden years for nothing. With the proper retirement coaching, you'll be able to create the retirement you dream of. In the following pages of this book, you'll learn how to proceed in this bright new pathway. If you're ready to take that first step toward your personal glory days, flip the page.

Chapter One

Accumulation Advisors Are Not Retirement Planners

If all the economists were laid end to end,

they'd never reach a conclusion. ~ George Bernard Shaw

There are two basic types of retirement advisors. Before you can find the right one for you, it is important to understand the difference between them. I've noticed a consistent misunderstanding in this area. Most people, when they seek medical advice, have no problem understanding the concept of specialization. You don't go to an orthodontist for a heart problem. But when it comes to financial planning, the impression most have is that all financial advisors are cut from the same bolt of cloth. Nothing could be further from the truth. An example of this is what happened to me a few years ago during my Mizpah induction ceremony into Shriners International, a fraternal organization widely known for its charity work with children's hospitals. While I am restricted by confidentiality oaths about revealing much of this ceremony, I can tell you this much. As part of the getting acquainted process, new inductees are given the opportunity to stand before the older members and tell the group a little about themselves. When I rose to do so, an interesting thing happened. I was asked what I did for a living. I explained that I was a financial advisor, and, before I could finish, I was interrupted with a few "boos" and some snickering. One gentleman went so far as to say that people in my profession were the cause of all of his financial woes.

Needless to say, this reaction upset me greatly. It also was an awakening of sorts. If that was his opinion about financial advisors, then perhaps many others had the same perception. The outspoken gentleman, I learned later, had a sizable portion of his portfolio invested in the stock market when it crashed in 2008. He and millions of others saw chunks of their life savings disappear overnight. Some of these individuals were young enough to earn and save their dollars back. Some were so wealthy they didn't even feel the pinch. But by far the vast majority of the people who were hurt by that financial disaster were those who were ill prepared to lose such a significant portion of their savings. Of course, few of these individuals managed their own money. Most of them had it parked with companies whose officers' business cards read…yep, you guessed it… "Financial Advisor."

No wonder this gentleman reacted the way he did. From his perspective, I was one of those people who lost him all that money in 2008! He was of the impression, mistaken though it was, that all financial advisors are **risk-oriented** financial advisors – the kind who focus more on the return **on** the money than the return **of** the money. From his point of view, and I suspect that of many others, all financial advisors are alike. I couldn't blame him for his misconception. Many in our profession don't make a distinction when they sit down with clients as to whether they work on the risk side or on the safety side of financial coaching. The media certainly hasn't done a thorough job of making the distinction between *risk-oriented* financial advisors and *safe-money* financial advisors.

Accumulation Planners and Retirement Planners

There is a big difference between **accumulation planners** and **retirement planners.** I coined these terms to assist you in recognizing the difference amongst financial advisor specialists. You won't find these terms in an industry textbook.

Accumulation advisors are in the majority. They evolved during the bull run of the 1980s and 1990s, and is probably the person you're working with today if you're still in the pre-retirement stage of life. During the accumulation phase of your life, you are working and earning, and hopefully saving and investing. These advisors help with your investments. As your retirement funds grew, they positioned them appropriately enough in the stock market, where they would have the best opportunity to grow. There was risk there, sure. But it was not inappropriate for your age to assume that risk. You had time on your side. The objective was for your money to steadily replicate itself as you added to it. One day, when the time was right, you would collect your last paycheck, wave goodbye to the workday, and allow that nest egg to fund your retirement. Phrased like that, it sounds like maybe there is a transition that should occur in your saving and investing pattern as you approach retirement. Well, guess what...*THERE IS!*

Appropriately, you invested for growth, using stocks, bonds, mutual funds, real estate investment trusts, options, maybe even variable annuities. You assumed the risk that accompanied these investment choices. The job of your advisor was to grow your assets at risk levels appropriate to your age and your risk tolerance until, one day, you ease off the risk pedal, put the brakes on, and make a major change in direction. You tell your beloved broker, who has done such a great job getting you to where you are today, that you appreciate the service and now you are no longer willing or able to assume as much risk as you previously did. You are now in a position where you must depend on your savings for daily expenses. You will "write your own paycheck," so to speak, from your retirement nest egg. These assets must be preserved and carefully distributed, not placed at undue risk for the purposes of growth. It is at this point that you explain to your accumulation advisor that you are now in need of three things: *safety, preservation of assets,* and *dependable income.*

All seems to be going well. Your advisor says, "Sure, we can do that! Let's restructure." Your advisor then proceeds to reallocate your assets, putting you into bond funds, variable annuities, and fixed income investments. But wait a minute. Your assets are still at risk! It seems your advisor is trying to help, but it still doesn't feel quite right. You're looking for words like "guarantee" and "safe" and you're hearing words like "projection" and "probable." To be perfectly candid, it's time to find a different advisor – one who specializes in retirement planning...one whose sole focus is working with individuals who are at or near retirement.

Suzie and the Salesman

We can compare the process mentioned above to the process of shopping for a new car. Suzie is young, unmarried, and just starting her career. She doesn't have a huge income but she needs a car to drive back and forth to work. Her priorities are:

Affordability – No payments for 12 months.
Gas Mileage – High 30s at least.
Compact – Needs to fit in a small garage.

Suzie walks into the dealership and meets John, the car salesman. Suzie explains what she's looking for and John says, "I am highly trained and very experienced, and I know exactly what you need." Suzie thinks to herself, "This salesman seems to be sensitive to my needs and knows exactly what he is talking about; maybe this will work." John then proceeds to show her a big, black Hummer H1, the biggest, baddest Hummer money can buy. Suzie, who is now starting to question the salesman's judgment, says, "It's beautiful, but I have a small garage and it certainly won't fit." John says, "Not a problem. I have a great relationship with a contractor who focuses solely on garages."

Suzie, starting to suspect that maybe the salesman just isn't catching on, tells him that 15 miles per gallon it isn't exactly fuel efficient, and she can't afford the cost of the Hummer H1, let alone the cost of constructing a new garage in which to park it. John, still scrambling for a solution, says, "Now I know what you need." He takes Suzie over to the smaller Hummer H3. Suzie is getting frustrated. She wonders why this salesman isn't listening. Why is he trying to sell her a four-wheel drive monster with a $40,000 price tag – still way outside her price range? But John tells her not to worry. "Suzie, we are running a special this month," he tells her. "You won't be required to make any payments for a full 12 months!"

Suzie, now discouraged and puzzled, heads for the door. But after she leaves the dealership, she looks up and sees the sign. The words "Hummer Dealership" are spelled out clearly in large block letters that measure at least two feet tall. Now she understands why the salesperson offered her a Hummer. Hummers were all he had to sell.

Seeking advice from a financial advisor whose scope is limited to only the accumulation side of the financial world is likely to produce the same results Suzie got. And unfortunately, in the financial advisory world, the signs usually aren't as easy to spot. The story about Suzie and the Hummer dealer may be a bit outlandish, but it's not all that different in substance from some I've heard from retirees and pre-retirees when they describe their experiences with the financial advisor with whom they worked. They reached that zone where they needed safety and income, but their current advisor only knew accumulation. They continued getting risk with all the bells and whistles. It's not the advisor's fault. He's doing everything he knows how to do, but risk is all he knows

Recognizing the Difference

Looking for the right financial advice can be harder than finding Waldo if you don't know what to look for. Look at it this way. You're interviewing candidates to determine whom you will select to be your personal "retirement doctor." As with any interview process, you'll be able to make a more intelligent choice if you listen carefully to what comes out of the interviewee's mouth. If you are dealing with an accumulation specialist, you'll hear certain words and expressions. You will likely be told these three things in the following order:

Return: You may hear them say, "This investment should return 7% per year." Or, "This mutual fund has returned 6% per year over the last 10 years." There is a strong focus on year-over-year returns rather than income.

Safety: After you hear about the return, your natural reaction is to ask how safe that investment is. You may hear them discuss the assets on the balance sheet, their diversification across sectors, the experience of the investment team, or how long they have been in business.

Income: Lastly, you hear about the income, yield, or dividends that are produced. You may hear expressions such as: "It has a 5% dividend yield." Or, "This mutual fund has created 4% per year in income." Please note that income is usually the last thing discussed in this dialogue, when, in retirement situations, it should be the first thing on the list.

On the other hand, when you listen to a Retirement Specialist you will hear about these three things in the following order…

Income: You will hear about _guaranteed_ retirement income, yield, or dividends. The most important thing in retirement is guaranteed income, so shouldn't that be what is discussed first when it comes to your investments?

Safety: You will hear about the Legal Reserve System, the guarantees provided, and how those guarantees are backed.

Return: Lastly, return is discussed. The return on your investments, not the assets you require to support your lifestyle. My father is fond of this expression: "It's not the return **on** your money that is critical in retirement; it is the return **of** your money."

Listen for these expressions and use them as a gauge to determine whether your advisor, or potential advisor, is on the accumulation side or the retirement side of advising. Your retirement advisor's job is not to make you rich, but to do everything in his power to make sure you will **_never be poor!_**. Once you determine which type of advisor is sitting on the other side of the table, you can easily determine if a second meeting is worthwhile.

Chapter Two

Achieving Financial Fitness

You don't bench-press 250 pounds on your first day. ~ *Anonymous*

Yogi Berra is said to be the king of malapropism – sayings that make sense in a nonsensical way. One of my favorites is, "You have to be careful if you don't know where you're going, you might just end up there." Those kinds of phrases make you shake your head and say, "What?" But it's clear what the old Yankee baseball catcher meant, isn't it? You simply must know what your ultimate destination is in life before you can successfully reach it. That especially is true when it comes to our financial futures. Where do you want to go, financially speaking?

When you look at it for what it really is, money amounts to just so many numbers printed on paper unless it has a purpose in your mind. When you zip open that envelope that contains the statement for your retirement account, it's just numbers. Look in your wallet. Numbers on paper accompanied with some Latin mottos and phrases and a portrait of a famous patriot. Money only takes on real meaning when we assign it a task. Pay my bills. That's a task. Buy food and a place to live. Keep me from becoming a burden to my children when I get older. That's a major task. Statistics bear out that one of the most poignant fears of those entering retirement is running out of money. It ranks higher than death or public speaking, believe it or not. But it's not the numbers on the paper that are important. It's the independence money can provide. That's what's truly meaningful. So, dear reader, I want you to take some time, if you haven't done so already, to focus on who you are and what your goals are. What exactly do **you** want **your** money to do for **you?**

All too often, when those seeking financial advice sit down with the advisor, they look expectantly to him or her for immediate recommendations. That's a little like going to a new doctor and expecting him to immediately prescribe a remedy without first doing an examination. Doctor's examinations usually start with the basics about your health. Your height, your weight, your blood pressure. Looking into your eyes, your mouth, your ears and checking your reflexes. Likewise, a competent financial advisor – especially one who specializes in retirement planning – will not recommend any course of action until he or she first gets to know who you are wealth-wise and what your financial goals are. You can help that process along a bit by doing some soul-searching in advance.

In the next few paragraphs we will explore how you define yourself. What does risk mean to you? What are your spending habits, your savings habits, what is your lifestyle? What are your legacy wishes – that is, what do you wish to leave behind for your loved ones once you "shuffle off this mortal coil" (Shakespeare). Setting goals must embrace these aspects of your attitude toward your assets before any effective planning can take place.

My grandfather Ralph Bailey was fond of the old saying, "God gave us two ears and one mouth for a reason." He was, of course, promoting the virtues of listening. A competent and effective financial advisor will start by simply listening to you as you relate your dreams, goals, wants, fears, desires, dreams, wishes.

"Who Am I?" Goal Setting

Because you are the only person who can truly define your goals, you must first ask yourself, "Who am I?" After all, how could you be expected to determine what you want to do in the future without first establishing a clear picture of where you are today?

Please pause for a second, stop reading, and think about who you are. Not your name, or what kind of car you drive, or what your annual income is, but who you really are deep down inside. Ask yourself, "What does money really mean to me?" I'll go first. To me, money means family. Money allows me to spend more time with my family. It allows me to buy the things my family needs to survive, such as food, shelter, and clothing. Money gives me and my family a sense of well-being and security.

Your answer may be different. But once you figure out who you are, you'll be able to discover for yourself what you want your money to do for you. Then, and only then, should you take the next step toward finding the perfect advisor for your retirement years.

It is my observation the answer to that question, "Who am I?" is ingrained in us over the years and eventually becomes fairly static. Let me ask you a question, and I want you to be totally honest with yourself when you answer it. Let's pretend you were a prescient being and could predict the stock market behavior over the next two years. Using your ability to foresee the future, you pick the next Google, or Microsoft, and your net worth doubles as a result. Scratch that. Since we're in a fantasy world here, let's say your net worth quadruples. Would that change in your financial status change the way you live your life? Would you start wearing high-priced designer clothing like Paris Hilton, traveling the world like Lemuel Gulliver, or showing off the latest Armani suit like Donald Trump? The honest answer is probably no. I've met multi-millionaires who still live in the same houses they lived in since they started out with nothing. Sure, you may splurge a bit now that you can afford it, but I doubt it will dramatically affect you.

But allow me to ask you a different question. Take your net worth, the value of all of your worldly possessions, and cut that value in half. Did that change the way you live your life? Of course it did! A lot of people who survived the market crash of 2008 would tell you that such a seismic economic jolt will most certainly transform your life. If nothing else, it produces higher stress levels. Experts confirm that stress brought on by such financial woes can affect you physically, actually shortening your life span. You would likely cut back on extravagances like expensive vacations, shopping trips (or at least you would be more judicious about what items you selected), restaurant dining, and entertainment. You may even find yourself watching your energy consumption more closely to lower utility bills.

So when you're contemplating what is most important to you, think seriously if it is about doubling your money, buying a new sports car, or a new Armani suit, or if it is about spending more quality time with your grandchildren, traveling with your spouse to places you always wanted to visit, or perhaps even giving back to the community. Maybe it's merely having the means to enable you to simply relax when you retire and not worry. Retirement planning isn't about asking when the stock market will give you your next classic car or fancy watch; it's about spending with confidence, often with a focus on the simpler things in life.

I've worked with people from every walk of life – doctors, attorneys, business people, teachers, and blue-collar savers – and the one thing I've found in all of these individuals is an interest in reducing stress and focusing on the important things in life when they retire. The MOST important things to all of these individuals is not to buy their next hot rod or travel around the world, but to insure that they never have to go back to work and will never be poor. While there is nothing wrong with hoping for the next home run with a portion of your portfolio to buy the convertible you've always wanted, it is critical that you know what money can be spent on your "fun" goals, and what money needs to be preserved for a worry free retirement. You never want to be in the position at retirement where you must constantly monitor the stock market, keeping track of its every movement. If you manage your portfolio with a purpose, securing the income you will need to support a comfortable retirement and only risking what you can afford to lose, then you will experience a truly stress-free retirement unleashing the true power of your life savings.

If you were to complete this sentence: "I want my retirement to be filled with _____." I don't think you would write the word "money" on that line. I don't think we would answer "risk" either. Yet from where I watch the world, I see far too many putting their retirement assets at far too much risk and focusing far too much on the daily movements of their money. Why is that?

Am I a Risk Taker?

Just as retirement isn't for everyone, retirement *planning* isn't for everyone. There are some who enjoy taking risks. Like that little jolt of excitement that comes from – there's no better word for it – gambling. Experts say adrenaline rushes can be addictive.

Not everyone has agreed with my conservative approach, which has prompted a few to give me the label, "The dinosaur in the corner of your portfolio." Call me crazy, but I strongly believe that if you don't **need** to take the risk, you **shouldn't** take the risk…not, if you **can** take the risk, you **should** take the risk.

If you are a risk taker by nature, you are likely waiting for the next double-digit stock market return and are willing to let your hard-earned money ride the roulette wheel the stock market has become in recent years. Perhaps you feed on the adrenalin rush produced by "playing the market." There is nothing wrong with this, everybody needs a little excitement in their lives. Just don't forget to determine how much "excitement" is appropriate for you to avoid risking your whole retirement.

Conversely, if you're risk averse and possess a strong belief in the value of saving, then you're pleased with a reasonable return and would prefer not to be shocked by losses in your retirement portfolio. This is where you will find a night-and-day difference between the two primary types of advisors – the **accumulation** planners and **preservation or income-driven** specialists. If you are a risk taker, maybe you really aren't ready for retirement. If you aren't a risk taker, then maybe it's time to see a retirement planner focused on preservation and income driven investing.

What is Risk?

There is a degree of risk in anything that we do in life. When it comes to investing, that is true as well. Maybe that risk is as low as the end of the world as we know it, or as likely as the collapse of an investment bank. Don't let even the highest quality bonds or stocks deceive you; there is risk with every investment – especially in the equity and bond markets. But you must understand the level of risk and claims paying ability of the company issuing your investments.

Whether you consider yourself a moderate or aggressive investor, the truth is you probably are not as risk tolerant as you think you are, especially if you are in or near retirement. I had an appointment with a retired widow who came into my office after listening to our radio show that dealt with the topic of risk. When I stepped into the conference room for our meeting she had her brokerage statement sitting in front of her, and in the top right hand corner of the statement, appeared the words, "conservative growth." I asked her what she thought her risk tolerance was and she replied, "I am definitely conservative. I hate losing money. I can't stand even short-term losses." So, I then asked her what her planner told her she could expect to lose if we experienced a worst-case scenario, such as a repeat of the 2008 market crash. She went on to explain that her financial advisor never discussed the probability of a worst-case scenario, or what possible effect it could have on her retirement portfolio.

This is a huge gap in portfolio planning, and I see it repeatedly. If you're not asking this question, then it is time to step up to the plate and ask the tough questions! Your retirement advisor should have access to sophisticated software to analyze what could happen in a worst-case scenario. This is always one of the first things we analyze when examining potential clients' current investments. By using third-party software, we discovered that if we were to experience another 2008, this woman's portfolio could lose as much as 40% with a 99% confidence interval. This shocked her and it was definitely not what came to mind when she read the words "conservative growth" at the top of her statement. So where then can you position your retirement assets for safety, preservation, and income?

The Worlds of Money

In my opinion, there are two different worlds where you can position your retirement funds – only two! There is the world of *risk* and the world of *safety.* These two areas can further be defined as *"i-know-so-money"* and *"i-hope-so-money."* If you are retired, this "i-know-so-money" becomes the most important part of your retirement portfolio.

It is my observation that many retirees and pre-retirees have been brainwashed into believing risk is the only way to achieve their retirement dreams. I don't believe they are getting the whole story. There are only a few places today where we can allocate funds and protect your principal from loss. By contrast, thousands of places exist to place funds where they are subject to potential losses. Safe places include checking and savings accounts, fixed annuities, Certificates of Deposit, and government debt.

If your money isn't in one of the places on the safe-money list in the above paragraph, then your money isn't completely safe. Maybe your broker or advisor said something like, "Stock market returns *average* 10% per year." Well, that's a great story, isn't it? Let me tell you one of my own. Between the two of us, my wife and I run 25 miles per week. That's pretty good, right? But the truth is, I run only one mile per week and my wife runs the rest. I didn't tell you the whole story, and your advisor hasn't either.

The average return for the longest running stock market index is right around 10%. But the time frame we're discussing is critical to understanding that statement. This average is based on any 25-year time period since 1929. If your money is invested in the stock market and you experience a market crash, do you have 25 years to make up the losses to your retirement account? I didn't think so. The market doesn't always go up over long periods of time, either. For instance, on December 31, 1928, the Dow Jones Industrial Average closed at 248.48. On December 31, 1949, the Dow closed the year at 200.13, equivalent to a loss of 19.46%. On August 30, 1964, the Dow closed at 838.48. On August 27, 1982, the Dow closed at 883.47 – equivalent to a total return of a 5.37% return over what was almost 20 years. As you can see from these examples, the true average return of the stock market depends on what period you examine. This isn't an attempt to totally discount the merits of the stock market as a place where growth can occur. Not at all! What I am trying to illustrate is that you need to see the entire picture before you project what you could experience in the way of "average returns."

Don't let yourself be brainwashed by the idea that the only way to keep up with inflation is to be fully invested in the stock market. Not that you can ignore inflation. We'll talk more about that later. But consider the fact that your expenses may decrease as you age.

People typically spend less as they age. You will probably have fewer people living under your roof. You even eat less, or at least you should, so the experts tell us, as your metabolism slows down with age. The mortgage stands a good chance of getting paid off as the years go by. You will typically pay less in taxes with the benefits of higher deductions and less taxable income. If you were saving for retirement, that will cease, because you are here now! If you're like most folks, you'll slow down your spending on such things as entertainment, clothes, travel, and other semi-discretionary expenses. I actually have one client who is in his early 80s who has been with our firm since he was in his mid-60s. When we do his annual review, we prepare a graph to indicate how much he is spending in semi-discretionary expenses. He was surprised to see how much less he spends now in comparison to what he did 15 years ago, but he seems to lack nothing.

Why So Conservative?

I once met a couple who thought I was too conservative to work with so they went with a financial advisor who persuaded them that they needed to be 100% in the market (stocks, bonds, and mutual funds) *in order to keep up with inflation.* Jim and Jan, we will call them, were retired and in their early 70s when we met. They had amassed a small fortune worth $1.3 million. Social Security was $2,600 per month, plus a pension of $1,500 per month. They needed to draw an additional $3,000 per month from their investments to support their desired retirement lifestyle. That's less than 3% per year. Over the next couple of years they lost over 60% of what they worked for their whole lives, leaving them with around $600,000. Drawing out $3,000 per month was now 6% of their portfolio. They had to be more worried about running out of money, than keeping up with inflation. Simple math would show that if they could draw a nice enough map, and remember where they put that map, they could have buried their $1.3 million in the backyard and it would have lasted the rest of their lives at that rate, and maybe even their children's lives, regardless of inflation. Why would this couple ever place at risk any of their retirement assets, or at least those retirement assets needed to guarantee their $3,000 per month with inflation? It may take as little as $500,000 to guarantee the level of income they need for the rest of their lives. Then, and only then, should Jim and Jan take risks with their remaining retirement assets.

I do believe the market has the *potential* to give you a better return than most other asset classes, if you have a lot of time. It is still a "buy-and-hope" approach, however. There are no guarantees, even if an excessive amount of time is on your side. If you're a retiree or pre-retiree, you have probably spent the majority of your life riding the market rollercoaster. But you can no longer play that game now because of the time factor. When I discuss managed risk, I am discussing an approach to your "growth" money, not your "income" money. Your assets need to be well diversified and not static. Your assets need to be dynamically managed to take advantage of arbitrage opportunities in the market and, at the same time, hedge your risk during difficult times. If you're unsure whether you're utilizing an actively managed risk philosophy, or a "buy-and-hope" approach, I encourage you to go back and look at what your portfolio did in 2008. This was a painful time for most static or basic strategic asset allocation portfolios. I ask about 2008 in every one of my first meetings with potential clients. I often get the deer-in-the-headlights look. Almost always I hear, "I lost money," or "I lost a substantial amount of money," or "I lost money and so did everyone else." I have to tell you, the last one drives me absolutely insane! If you believe this to be true, then you have been brainwashed by the market-based financial advisors in the investment world that **everybody** loses when the market goes down. It simply isn't true. We both know that, no matter the game, there is always a winner and a loser. I can prove it.

We take the first step down this path by looking at several investments that did quite well in 2008. In 2008, long-term government bonds, for example, returned an average 22.5%. Money markets returned roughly 2%. ProShares Short S&P 500 ETF returned 24.01%. Wal-Mart Stores, Inc. (WMT) was up 15.12%. SPDR Gold Trust (GLD) was up 3.16%. Dollar Tree, Inc. (DLTR) rose 65.18%. Panera Bread Co (PNRA) gained 55.89%. I could go on and on. So this begs the question, then, why were we told that **everyone** lost money in 2008? Surely there were people out there with the experience and presence of mind to know that it was time to move into bonds.

But why did the majority of people lose money in 2008? It all had to do with the philosophy that many brokers and advisors utilized. They were still focused on the old money management techniques of the 80s and 90s called Strategic Asset Allocation, a buy-and-hold strategy drawn from Modern Portfolio Theory that we'll discuss in later chapters.

(Long-Term Government Bonds – VUSTX Vangard Long-Term Treasury Fund, Money Market - VMPXX – Vanguard Treasury Money Market Fund. Returns will vary dependent on index utilized. Returns of Exchange Traded Funds and stocks can be found at finance.yahoo.com)

The Suggestion of 100

So how much risk should you have in your retirement portfolio? Many advisors suggest you follow the "Rule" of 100." The formula goes like this: Just take your age and subtract it from 100. What's left is the percentage of your assets you should have at risk. If you're 75 years old, then 75% of your assets should be positioned in accounts backed by a legal reserve system, or "safe" assets. The other 25% of your assets should be positioned in risk-based investments, including stocks, bonds, real estate, etc.

Frankly, I am appalled by the mere suggestion of a "rule" here. Advisors have used this tactic for years to instill fear in retirees and to sell the products they are biased toward, the only products they have available, the products that pay the highest commission, or the products their corporate office pushes. But this is wrong.

There is no all-encompassing rule; there is only YOU and YOUR money. The amount of your retirement that should be in either a position of safety or a position of risk is different for each of us. I am going to pass along to you what I think is the best rule of thumb that can be used for arriving at the proper balance of safety and risk. It happens to be one instilled in me by my grandfather Howard when I was a young lad. It goes like this: "Never risk more than you can afford to lose." Somewhere along the way, we seem to have lost touch with this simple, commonsense advice. Or maybe we have merely been brainwashed and misled by advisors with alternative agendas.

What is the money you cannot afford to lose? It is the money you depend on for your survival. It's the block of assets that create the income you will need for the rest of your life. Determine this number, and you will have at the same time determined the appropriate amount of money you may place at risk during your retirement.

What Do You Mean Conservative?

Let me warn you that, on top of all of this, believe it or not, your advisor may have a completely different idea of what risk is than you do. From my point of view, this is one of the first things you should determine when interviewing your new retirement advisor. They will most likely have you fill out a *risk tolerance* questionnaire, which is supposed to magically tell them exactly how to allocate your funds.

Do you think it is really possible to determine your financial goals and needs from a questionnaire? You are more than a page full of check boxes. The easy way to find out where your potential advisor stands when it comes to risk is to ask him or her how much he or she feels you could stand to lose in a down market, such as 2001 or 2008. If they have been around for a while, perhaps they will be able to even show you those historical returns on paper. If you're wondering whether your current portfolio aligns with your idea of the proper level of risk, ask your advisor to run some simulations. An experienced advisor will have access to sophisticated software with the ability to illustrate probabilities of different degrees of loss. Determining the level of risk you are comfortable taking with your hard-earned assets is a key step toward making the right decision on your "retirement doctor."

Repurposing Your Investments

Every investment in the world has a specific purpose for which it was created. Make sure your investments are most efficiently accomplishing your goals.

Bank	Dividend Income Strat.	Growth Strategies
Fixed Annuities	Preferred Stock	Small Cap Stock
Hybrid Annuities	Senior Secured Loans	Options
Government Bonds	Dividend Stocks	Growth Stocks
	Invst. Grade Bonds	Futures
	REITs	Commodities
	Master L.P.	Currencies
		Emerging Markets

Basic Living Income — **"Fun" Income** — **Growth & Inflation Protection**

Low — Spectrum of Risk — High

Casey Weade

Chapter Three

Purpose-Based Budgets and Goal Setting

*The great and glorious masterpiece of man is to know
how to live to purpose. ~ Michel de Montaigne*

Before you ever get to retirement, you should have a budget that identifies what you spend and where you spend it. Before you ever set your retirement goals, you should know your habits. Habits will assist you in developing a better self-awareness, leading to a higher level of goal setting. I have had a budget from a young age. I first started with labeled envelopes. I wanted a new bicycle. I wanted to be able to go to the movies. I would take a portion from my allowance and a portion of my earnings doing odd jobs for neighbors and place those amounts in envelopes simply marked "BIKE" and "MOVIES." As I got older, I budgeted the same way for golf equipment, dates, greens fees, a new car, and, ever the responsible saver, my Roth IRA contribution. As I began to meet many of my financial goals and as my income improved, life became a bit more complicated. I was impelled to find better, more efficient ways of budgeting. These budgeting methods and strategies are more sophisticated than my envelope method, but it is essentially the same principle at work. Set the money aside. Once it is earmarked and put away, it is as good as spent. If you go over budget in one area, the only way to make that up is to take it from another envelope, or column, so your budget balances. Many great tools are available for budgeting today.

The number one question as you approach retirement should be, "How much income will I need when I retire?" I find that most folks who walk into my office have no idea what they are spending or what they are saving on an annual basis. This is an ***enormous*** gap in the organization of your finances. There are many "magic formulas" out there, such as the idea you'll need 60-80% of your pre-retirement income during retirement. Think thoroughly about this and it will come down to what your retirement goals are. I've seen some people who could make it on 25% of their pre-retirement income in retirement. I've also seen people who needed 150% of their pre-retirement income during their retirement. If that seems strange, just think about it for a minute. What do you plan to do in retirement? Do you plan to sit behind your desk all day and carry in lunch? Of course not! When you retire your free time explodes! Maybe you want to pick up golf or spend more time with your friends. In general, more free time equals more expenses. Focus on your goals and these numbers will come with budgeting and tracking.

Become a Money Tracker

What do I mean by tracking? I mean tracking every single penny you spend – from a pack of chewing gum you buy at the local convenience market to the mortgage payment you make every month. This has become much easier through Internet software technology. You can utilize computer programs that allow you to download all of your banking transactions directly to your computer. Some of these financial tracking programs even categorize your expenses. I recommend tracking your expenses for at least a year before you retire, so you can get a true feel of what your regular expenses are, and also your unexpected expenses. Once you see a spending pattern develop, you are ready to begin to make adjustments. Perhaps you can slim down on certain expenses and save more. You're on your way to creating a higher level of financial organization.

Take a close look at how your expenses will change once you reach retirement. Will your mortgage be paid off? Will your gas expenditures go down? Will you retire with health insurance? Or will you have to pay for your own health insurance until you qualify for Medicare? What kind of automobile will you drive? Are you likely to downsize your family home now that the kids are gone? What about legacy? What would you like to do for your children and grandchildren? Once you narrow these things down, it is time to live it. When I say live it, I want you to do it NOW. Don't wait to cut your income when you retire. Track your expenses for a year, develop your retirement budget, then put it into motion. Try living on the amount of income you think you will need during retirement for one year prior to retirement. This will show you exactly what living on that budget will mean. If you've never lived on a budget before, prepare yourself, because you are about to retire on a fixed income.

What Does Legacy Mean to You?

In my family, two ideals compete when it comes to legacy. On my mother's side, there has never been a financial legacy left behind. My maternal grandfather believes more in helping those he loves while he is still living than he does in leaving behind a large inheritance. At the time of this writing, he is 85 and still working, still giving, and still loving every minute of it. I attribute my positive mental attitude, my compassion, my spirit of gratitude, and most of what I have accomplished in life to my Grandfather Ralph. His legacy will be the all the people he has influenced, both financially and emotionally; he will live on in those whose lives he touches. Maybe you've heard the saying, "I plan to spend my last dime and write a bad check right before they put the nails in the coffin." Is there anything wrong with this? Absolutely not! From my way of thinking, he'll leave behind something no one can put a price tag on and something which money could never buy. But unlike my grandfather, most people do have measurable monetary goals and aspirations regarding the legacy we wish to leave behind for the next generation.

On my father's side, it's a different story entirely. My great-grandfather left a little bit behind for my grandfather, who had a goal of leaving a little more for his children. My father plans to leave a little more than that behind for me, and I plan to leave that and add to it for my children. We all have a strong sense of family and have seen the benefits that come from leaving something behind for the next generation. This mode of thinking engendered a caring spirit and enabled each successive generation to enhance the basic quality of life for the ones ahead. Financial security and measurable wealth is not all that my Grandfather Howard left behind. He also left me with a strong work ethic and an understanding of what it means to learn by earning and to keep what one earns.

Perhaps a financial legacy isn't something that matters that much to you. But it is a piece of the retirement puzzle you need to recognize and put into place. During client interviews, I've come across many who say they see no need to leave anything of substance behind. If this is the case with you, then perhaps you would be wise to maximize your income today. Why spend any less than you know you can? There are financial products in this world today that will guarantee that you never run out of money. I've seen investment vehicles that can guarantee withdrawal rates of as high as 8% on your retirement assets for the rest of your life. If you have no desire to leave anything behind, and you desire to spend the money you earned, then why not guarantee that income and enjoy it as you have planned to do?

I saw a bumper sticker on the back of a large recreational vehicle the other day that read: "We are spending our children's inheritance." At five miles per gallon, I believe that inheritance is literally going up in exhaust smoke. One couple told me they would love to leave something behind for their children, but there really was no need to. Both the son and the daughter obtained master's degrees, one in engineering and one in medicine. They were both financially well taken care of through their own efforts. The couple made sure they gave their children a good education, and the rest was something they achieved through their own efforts. How could anyone not applaud that way of thinking?

"We are going to enjoy our money as long as we are healthy and able to travel," she said. "And then we have a couple of charities we intend to leave it to."

I second that emotion. Believe it or not, there are financial strategies to enable that type of retirement goal and even guarantee* it in a tax-advantaged manner. There are also ways of creating guaranteed tax-free rates of return for the next generation if it is something you desire. Extensive estate planning can be done to ensure the next generation is left with opportunities you never had.

---

*(All guarantees are based on the financial strength and claims-paying ability of the issuing insurance company, who is solely responsible for all obligations under its policies.)

When it comes to legacy, there is no wrong answer. It is prudent, and just good retirement planning, however, to determine which type you are. That will help you further define the answer to the question at hand: Who is the right "retirement doctor" for me?

Can I Do It Myself?

Are you a do-it-yourselfer? I see nothing wrong with that. Perhaps you're one of those people who get a sense of pride out of planning for yourself. While that's understandable, I must issue a word of caution here. Tread carefully. When you get into the nuts and bolts of retirement planning, there are a few areas where you will probably need professional help. I'm sure none of us in sound mind will be practicing self-dentistry anytime soon. I know of a few people who practice self-medication, particularly on the weekends, but that doesn't seem to make for good results. Besides, retirement planning will more than likely involve activities for which you will need either a securities license, or an insurance license, or both in order to stay within the law.

Over the years, I've observed many competent and successful individuals manage their own retirement but complain they still have a sense that money is falling through the cracks. These individuals often surround themselves with experts. They are able to obtain professional advice from their insurance agent, their stock broker, their CPA, and their attorney, etc. But even with that team behind them, they still feel money falls through the cracks somehow. Could it be that they need a "quarterback" whose job is to see the entire playing field? Would it help if they had someone to "conduct the orchestra," so to speak, and make sure all the instruments are in tune?

Some are fanatics about online trading. This phenomenon appeared on the scene in the mid-1990s with the advent of faster personal computers and the Internet. My feelings are a bit mixed about this one. I know folks who seem to live their lives behind the computer screen, watching the ticker symbols bounce around. They pay attention to every little blip and don't seem to be able to even take a walk without worrying what is happening on that little screen. That's no way to live, if you ask me. I've also heard horror stories about losses they incurred by misjudging the meaning of those ubiquitous charts and graphs. Those tell history, not the future…a lesson some learned the hard way.

All that having been said, there are still people who love online trading. I've met some individuals who find this activity to be one of the most pleasurable things about having free time in retirement. I even know seniors who started an online investment club. They're computer savvy and have allocated a portion of money they dubbed their "play money," an agreed upon amount each year that's never more than $5,000. They have fun because there is no stress, and any losses they experience don't come out of money they must have in order to survive.

On the other hand, one man I know of – we'll call him Jack – was an ardent saver and managed every nickel of it by himself. Jack started his do-it-yourself portfolio management way before the days of online trading. He had ledger books organized by year and account. He phoned in buy/sell orders to his broker (the only way you could do it in those days) and tracked the market by means of the newspaper's financial page. You can imagine his glee when, in the mid-1990s, organizations like Scottrade and Compuserve began allowing account holders to click a few buttons and buy and sell stocks from the privacy of their own home. He was cautious at first, but by 1997 he was "all in," as they say in poker. He placed his entire life savings in three accounts that offered online trading. Electronic charts produced by such analysts as Morningstar and StockCharts gave him real-time status reports on his positions. He was happiest when he was behind his computer buying and selling. Tech stocks were Jack's favorite. It was as though any company with a dot-com on the end was a darling. During what is now referred to as the "dot com boom," these stocks knew only one direction – up. Then, toward the end of the 1990s, the horizon began to darken for information technology stocks, most of which were traded on the Nasdaq Stock Exchange. The speculative bubble that started in 1997 peaked in 2000, when the Nasdaq composite index hit 5,132.52. It bottomed in March of 2001, falling to 1,923.64. On the heels of that, the overall stock market took a tumble resulting in the loss of $5 trillion in corporate value. Jack lost more almost three-fourths of his retirement nest egg.

A year later, Jack suffered a massive heart attack and died at 68 years of age. His wife of 43 years knew nothing of computers and had no clue as to how to retrieve what was left of their savings.

There is nothing wrong with online trading, but it can be treacherous, even if you're a fully trained professional. By all means, have a plan in place for what will happen when you are gone. You'll want to have an advisor lined up to help your family.

I am constantly on the lookout for new products because, just like automobiles, financial products change constantly. Every year, it seems, something new appears on the scene. From year to year, I will use a different company with different product guarantees depending on what changed. Keeping up with this ever-moving scene requires paying constant attention to trade journals, emails, webinars, and the streaming information released by wholesalers who design and sell these concepts. I attend educational conferences several times a year just so I can stay up to date on the latest developments in the financial market. I spend hours a week reading to stay current, sifting through hundreds of articles in dozens of publications that appear in the mail stack. As a Certified Financial Planner™™, I am required to complete 30 hours of continuing education every two years. Tack onto that the 24 hours of CE every two years required by the department of insurance in each state where I hold a license, and the additional five hours each year to maintain my long-term care certification, and you can see all that is involved in simply staying current. I also have an extensive network of financial advisors with whom I work. That keeps me on top of my game too. The workload itself is daunting. I work with anywhere from five to 15 portfolios per week, conducting annual reviews and providing financial evaluation.

In addition to keeping current personally, it is vital to keep up with technology. Along those lines, I keep access to sophisticated software designed to assist in the building of financial plans that have varying degrees of complexity. I tell you all of this not to toot my own horn, but to illustrate how much is involved with merely staying up to date in the field of retirement planning. So if you intend on doing it on your own, make sure you are prepared for the task you're taking on.

It's Time to Dream

If you've taken your time, paused here and there to reflect, then you should have developed a clearer understanding of who you are and what you want out of your retirement. Now it's time to dream a little.

Brian Tracy, in his book *Eat that Frog,* says goals are the fuel in the furnace of achievement. I believe that. My parents always set goals and encouraged me to do the same. I am living proof that if you practice proper goal-setting techniques, then you will certainly attain those goals.

One of my first financial goals was to accumulate $10,000 in my Roth IRA by the time I graduated high school. With CDs at the bank, pinching pennies, and hard work I was able to accumulate more than this by the time I went to college. I had a goal of becoming a Certified Financial Planner™™ by age 24. I did it with a year to spare. I had a goal of buying my first Mercedes by age 25; I did it by age 24. Did I attain all of my goals? No. That's the magic of goal setting. If you aim for the center of the target, you may not hit the center every time, but you are likely to be closer than if you didn't aim. Goals have to be specific but you must be flexible. For example, in the fifth grade I was becoming a pretty good golfer. I had a goal to play varsity golf in ninth grade, and I accomplished that goal. But I have yet to win, or even play in, The Masters, the greatest golf tournament. You must always have stretch goals along with your short-, medium-, and long-term goals.

Goal setting is utilized by successful businesspeople, athletes, and achievers in all walks of life. If we think of goals as the stair steps that led to our current success, then we may feel that once we reach retirement we can stop setting and achieving goals. But goals are like a compass. They keep us on course, pointed in the right direction. Retirement is not the end of our life journey. Some may argue that it's merely the beginning. As long as a ship is moving, it will rely on its compass to guide the way. You must continue setting goals in order to see forward progress.

Earlier, I told you about my father who retired in his early 50s, planning to play golf the rest of his life. One of the reasons that didn't work out for him and he returned to work, was a sense of accomplishment was missing. Setting meaningful goals and achieving them is the juice that makes some of us tick. Doing nothing has proven to be anathema to the generation known as "Baby Boomers." They, more than any generation before them, have eschewed the image of the rocking chair and knitting needles that characterized retirement in the days of their forefathers (please, no letters from the American Rocking Chair Association or Knitters Unanimous – both are fine activities). Modern retirees seem to be more driven to go and do. Some learn new hobbies. Others start new businesses. You have been setting goals your whole life to get to the glory land called retirement. Once you get there, you may find it useful to continue setting goals as a way to remain energized and progressive.

Getting Started

First, look at the "big picture" of what you plan to do with your retirement years, and try to pinpoint what you would like to achieve. Perhaps your goals will involve family. If you're the type who works with your hands, you may want to build a tree house for your grandchildren. Or, if you don't have grandchildren, then you may have in mind putting that woodworking shop in your garage – the one you always told yourself you would put together but never had the time. Neither of those things may even remotely interest you, but you get the idea. Think of things you would enjoy doing that may require a timeline and step-by-step moves to accomplish.

Your goal may involve a charity. Draw a clear mental picture of what you could do to pay back to the community in some way. Perhaps you're a professional who would reap satisfaction from offering "pro bono" work to a worthwhile cause now that you have time. Perhaps it is a monetary goal that could be achieved through some public effort, such as a walk for muscular dystrophy or fun run for cancer. Would you perhaps enjoy organizing garage sales or scrap drives to help wounded war veterans? Can you see yourself getting involved with fund-raising activities for worthy causes? The possibilities are endless.

Perhaps friends are your focus. Are there certain relationships you enjoyed before retirement that you would now like to cultivate by spending more time with individuals with whom you have a lot in common? Do you have friends who live a few states away that have invited you to visit them, but you declined because in your working years you lacked the time? Would it give you a focus on the future to list them and plan the trips?

As you think about these things, it may be useful to think about the "why" part of it. Why do you want to spend more time with family, friends, or engage in more charitable activities? What do you get out if it? If it's simply good feelings that go along with accomplishing any worthwhile goal, then that feeling will motivate you.

I've have found that breaking lifetime goals, or major goals, down into smaller goals will help you reach them. If your goal is to lose 20 pounds, you do it day at a time. If you goal is to compile your memories into a book about your family, you do it page at a time.

I love the story Zig Ziglar tells about goal setting. One of my favorite lines from *See You at the Top* is: "By the mile it's a trial…but by the inch it's a cinch." Ziglar recommends the "disciplined application of doing something every day to reach your objectives in life." He gives the following example:

"Losing 37 pounds in 10 months meant that I lost an average of 1.9 ounces per day. Writing a 384-page book in 10 months meant that I wrote an average of 1 1/4 pages per day."

Any grand adventure, such as a trip with the grandkids to Disney, starts with a kernel of thought – that's a goal. You can set goals in all areas of your life – finance, education, family, arts, attitude, physical fitness, pleasure, public service. Spend time brainstorming and reflecting. Select one or two goals in each category listed that best reflect the ultimate goal you're attempting to achieve.

Once you determine your lifetime goals, set a five-year plan of smaller goals that you need to complete to reach your ultimate goal. Then create a one-year plan, six-month plan, and a one-month plan of ever smaller goals that you need to achieve. Make sure they're specific. For example, to say "I want to take the family to Disney" is not as powerful as to say, "I want to take the family to Disney by (fill in exact month, day and year)." Set realistic goals that are attainable within a specific time frame.

When you go through this process, you'll find your goals are actually not focused on money, the stock market, or next year's home run. Instead they are focused on what is truly important to you in retirement. Once you've determined this, you can take the next step toward finding the right advisor for you.

Questions to ask yourself:

- After your retirement years have passed and you have left this world, what would you have hoped your life savings accomplished for you?

- Do I desire to leave money behind for the next generation? What do I want my legacy to be?

- Do I want to help my friends and family members, financially, during my retirement years?

- Which do I want – the potential for high returns or reasonable returns with peace of mind?

- How will I pay for healthcare during retirement?

- Do I have specific travel goals?

- Do I have charitable ambitions? What impact do I want to have in other's lives?

- Where do I want to live during retirement?

- What kind of car do I want to drive?

- Do I have an unfulfilled passion?

- How would I spend my time if I had more of it?

- If I had only a few months to live, what would I do?

Chapter Four

There Is No Silver Bullet – Repurposing Your Investable Assets

I believe that if you show people the problems and you show them the solutions they will be moved to act. ~ Bill Gates

Now that you've set goals, it is time to take the first step toward achieving them. In this chapter, I will teach you the simplest, and yet single most important, planning concept you will ever learn.

Have you ever been to Mexico or the Caribbean, and experienced one of those amphibious boat rides? My wife and I did. The attraction was called the "Amazing Amphibious Bus Tour." The Cayman Islands, located in the British West Indies, are known for clear blue water, powdery white sand beaches, and great snorkeling. For our one-year anniversary, we decided to purchase tickets to ride on what looks like a large bus with gigantic windows that tours the city of George Town one minute and splashes into turquoise water the next. It was a fun trip and an interesting ride, but there are tradeoffs to riding in a bus that does double duty as both a boat and a bus. As clever and entertaining as our tour guide was, he could do little about the fact that the bus was slow. He could also not improve our comfort level. Even though the boat was labeled "unsinkable" because of the strategic insertion of foam in sections of the bus/boat's undercarriage, we were still afloat in a road vehicle that, for all the reassurance given us by the our driver/captain, seemed unseaworthy.

The amphibian bus, or hydra/terra, as some call it, reminds me of the financial strategies put in place by some financial advisors these days. Attempts to cobble together strategies that give you the best of both worlds often miss the mark completely.

Take variable annuities. These are thought by some financial planners to be the "silver bullet" that promises **all** the returns of the stock market with **none** of the risk. (My compliance department would like me to note that variable annuities are exposed to market risk, if you couldn't sense the sarcasm.) These "silver bullets" are marketed as the vehicle that will guarantee your income, protect your principal, and provide a hedge against inflation. A miracle! All your problems are solved! NO! If this one, single product is your retirement plan, think again, please.

The best way to structure your retirement plan without watering down your growth, income, and legacy potential is through what I call purpose-based planning. Lumping all of your assets into one single financial product, regardless of what product that it may be, and regardless of how many nifty things it may do, is a bit like forcing the proverbial square peg into a round hold. Purpose-based planning simply means carving your assets into special blocks of money and assigning them a purpose based on several factors, including liquidity, income, growth, and estate planning priorities. Creating a purpose for your assets comes first. Finding a vehicle to achieve that purpose is secondary. Placing your assets inside a product or a strategy without first assigning them purpose is putting the proverbial cart before the horse.

There is no one-size-fits-all product, strategy, or approach. No "silver bullet" product or investment vehicle will get you to your retirement goals in one swift and easy stroke. Each planning case is different because each individual is different. Each person's dreams, goals, and desires differ greatly from one to another.

You Need an Emergency Fund - Liquidity

Were you told by your parents and grandparents, "Don't forget to stash some cash for a rainy day"? They taught a smart strategy. Your emergency fund is the most vital part of your financial plan. An emergency fund is typically thought of as the money you can get if you have unexpected expenses, such as medical bills or home repairs. It can also mean funds you have on hand if you wish to help a friend or family member in case of need.

How much should you have in an emergency fund? There is no set amount. The answer to that question will depend largely upon your comfort zone. One rule of thumb is to have three to twelve months of your required income set aside in case you lose your job, for example. When you're young and have a family, you may need six months. As you get older and more financially stable, I recommend that you have at least a three-month emergency fund. Required income can be defined as money you need to survive – funds you need to purchase the necessities, such as food, shelter, and clothing.

Where should you keep your emergency fund? These assets don't have to all be kept in the bank. I recommend that you diversify but keep them liquid. You may even want to keep some of the money ultra-liquid. You may wish to keep three months worth of your cash under-the-mattress liquid. Then another three months can be kept in a bank, or money-market account. Then you can get creative with the other six months.

Managing your cash to keep it liquid and still get a decent return can be a challenge in low interest rate environments. In most cases, the return on short-term investments is disgustingly low. As of this writing, the average rate of return on a one-year certificate of deposit is less than one half of one percent. Factor in 3% inflation and it doesn't take a math wizard to see that you are losing 2 ½% per year. That's what I call a Certificate of Disappointment. There are other options, however, that any competent independent financial advisor should know about. There are certain types of life insurance, for example, that can be a great place for an emergency stash. These policies can guarantee returns of 3% or 4% and are indexed to the stock market without penalties for withdrawal. Just remember, your goal with an emergency fund is that it be readily available without a penalty. Structured correctly, a life insurance policy may be the perfect vehicle.

Your emergency stash is not just about a specific dollar amount. It is about having a plan to deal with the unexpected. Having such a contingency fund will prevent you from derailing your savings program. Without an emergency fund, you will be tempted to draw money from funds that are earmarked for retirement. More likely than not, those funds are earning compound interest. Money withdrawn from such an account results in a "double whammy" loss. You are not likely to replace the money, and you lose the interest you would have earned.

Guaranteed **Income** & The Legal Reserve System

If you've read this far, then you're aware of the most important part of your retirement plan ... INCOME! Once you have your emergency fund in place, it is time to focus on what will drive your retirement lifestyle. The income you will need for retirement, whether you're looking at a 20-year retirement or a 40-year retirement, should not be put at risk. It should not even be structured with long-term bonds. We saw what can happen when the rating agencies get it wrong, as they did in the case of Ford and Lehman Brothers in 2008. It should be structured with savings vehicles backed by a legal reserve system.

The legal reserve system requires by law that certain levels of funds be set aside and maintained at all times to cover future obligations of the issuing company. The FDIC is one example of a legal reserve system for banks, and it requires banks in the system to have certain minimum guaranteed reserves. However, not all reserve systems are created equal. Some require 100% reserves (dollar-for-dollar) to be kept in place. Other systems may require only a few pennies on each dollar of obligations. Certificates of Deposit, for instance, are backed by the legal federal reserves maintained by the Federal Deposit Insurance Corporation (FDIC). While the FDIC backs deposits up to $250,000 per Social Security number per institution, banks aren't required to keep 100% dollar-for-dollar legal reserves on hand to back up these deposits. Investments, such as stocks and bonds, don't carry reserve requirements, and that's one reason you may have seen some stocks and bonds become completely worthless throughout history.

Savings vehicles backed by a legal reserve system include banks, government bonds, and insurance companies. We've discussed banks and understand that the Federal Reserve can print its own money to back up government bonds, but how does an insurance company's legal reserve system operate? The easiest way to describe this is to compare the way they operate with the way the banking system works. Banks are required by the Board of Governors of the Federal Reserve System (FRB) to keep $8 on hand for every $100 they lend. This attributes to the colossal earnings power of the banking system. For example, when you give the bank $100,000, they can lend out $1,250,000. They may pay you 2% interest, and then extend loans to small businesses and individuals and charge them 8% interest. They are required to pay you $2,000 and are able to bring in $100,000. In my opinion, this is what led to the banking crisis of 2008.

I'm not saying banks aren't a safe place to put your money, since they are still backed by the FDIC, but it is interesting to compare banks with insurance companies when it comes to which ones are on the most solid footing when it comes to required reserves.

The states, rather than the federal government, regulate insurance companies. What significance does that have? Insurance companies are required to follow the guidelines of up to 50 states versus one entity, if they intend to operate nationally. This fact tends to make them more regulated, not less. Unlike banks, insurance companies must have a dollar in reserves for every dollar they have at risk. Banks are allowed to invest their working capital in a wide range of investments, ranging from mortgages and securities to small business loans, according to the Federal Reserve website.

Insurance companies, on the other hand, are required to keep the majority of their customer's funds in ultra-conservative investments, such as U.S. government bonds and highly rated corporate bonds. If they make more speculative investments, they must use their own capital, not the portion that is required by law to be set aside to settle customer claims.

The National Organization of Life and Health Insurance (NOLHGA) has stated that the fixed insurance industry is now better prepared than other areas of the financial industry to withstand national economic challenges. In the 18 months leading up to June of 2009, not a single life insurer had to be liquidated as a result of the economic downturn, NOLHGA documentation said. Furthermore, there has not been a single failure of a fixed insurance carrier of national significance since 1994. This is in stark contrast to the 62 bank failures from 2008 to June 2009.

Beyond its primary reserves, an insurance company further reduces risk through the use of surplus capital. Throughout my professional career I've found most insurance companies hold somewhere between 5% and 15% in excess reserves. I've even seen insurance companies with reserves in excess of 90%, or $190 on hand for every $100 they owe. When the surplus capital drops below minimums required by the state in which the company is located, the state may put the insurance company into receivership and take over. This is rare, but it has happened. When it does, the state takes over the legal responsibility to make sure client funds are transferred to a stronger insurance company as soon as possible. Client accounts of an insurance company are highly valuable, which is why, in most cases, a stronger insurance company is very willing to pay money to acquire those assets. What happens in the rare case where no buyer can be found to take over those assets? That's when reinsurers step into the picture.

Reinsurance is the process by which part or all of the insurer's risk is assumed by other companies in return for part of the premium paid by the insurer. Many primary insurers have purchased reinsurance from as many as 10 different companies. Even with all of these safety nets in place, it is still prudent to do your due diligence when placing your assets with an insurance company. Focus on the assets and investments of the insurance company before depositing your hard-earned dollars with them.

Reverse Dollar Cost Averaging (RDCA)

To reinforce why you should not be drawing your income from your investment portfolio, let's touch on the topic of Reverse Dollar Cost Averaging. If you've accumulated substantial retirement assets, then you probably benefited from the principles of Dollar Cost Averaging during your working years. Dollar Cost Averaging is a concept that takes advantage of the volatility of the stock market to reduce cost over time. If, for example, you had a 401(k) plan, 403(b) plan, 457 plan, or another qualified retirement plan at work, and you contributed to that plan at regular intervals over your working years, then you benefited from Dollar Cost Averaging. Here's how: Let's say you contributed $100 per month into your 401(k). That money was used to purchase shares of a mutual fund at whatever price those shares cost at the time of the contribution. When the share price goes up, **congratulations!** Your account balance just went up **and** you purchased fewer shares upon your contribution. When share prices drop, **congratulations!** Your $100 bought more shares at a lower price. This reduces your overall cost for investing into the market. It's a win/win situation. The two key ingredients are **regular** deposits made **over time.** (Disclosure: Dollar cost averaging is not a guarantee against market losses.)

But what happens when you retire. You are no longer **contributing** to your plan on a regular basis, you are **withdrawing** from your plan on a regular basis. When you withdraw money you are **selling** shares of that mutual fund. You are withdrawing much more per month than you were depositing during your working years. Whether share prices are up or down, you must withdraw the same amount per month. A market downturn can devalue the share price of that mutual fund and make your withdrawal twice as punitive. Let us take an example using the fictitious characters Dan and Kris. Dan and Kris retire with $1,000,000 and wish to draw 5% per year or $50,000 per year. Sounds doable right? Let's say they leave everything in the market and the year after they retire the bottom falls out of the market. Their account value loses 40% and is now worth $600,000. What rate of return will it take for them to get back to even? The answer is 66.67%. Do they still need their income? Of course they do! They are living on a fixed income and have bills to pay! So, they draw their $50,000 out of their portfolio. Now they have $550,000. Now what rate of return will it take to get back to even? The answer is 81.82%. Throw in inflation and that number could be even higher. If they could leave those dollars alone like they did in their working years it would in all likelihood come back, but they can't wait anymore. Reverse Dollar Cost Averaging is digging them a hole they will in all likelihood never get out of. It's easy to see why prudent investors, once they are no longer contributing to a 401(k) on a regular basis, move the money into an account that can provide a guaranteed income and one that cannot be affected by the vagaries of an unpredictable stock market. Using withdrawals from a tax-qualified market-based investment account to fund a retirement income is like sticking out your financial chin for a Reverse Dollar Cost Averaging knockout punch.

We violate the age-old investing discipline "sell high and buy low" when we don't change the way we invest our money when it is time to spend our money. Even if we don't need to withdraw money from qualified accounts such as IRAs and 401(k)s, we will be forced to take withdrawals referred to as Required Minimum Distributions (RMDs) when we turn 70 ½.

Take George and Donna, for example. They just reached the age when the IRS forces them to begin withdrawing funds from their retirement accounts. The formula used is based on IRS life expectancy tables. Withdrawals start at approximately 4% per year and increase gradually as you age. With their portfolio valued at $100,000, this is equivalent to $4,000 per year. The value you're forced to use in this process is the value of your qualified account on December 31 of the previous year. Unfortunately for George and Donna, they turned 70½ in 2007. The market crash of 2008 cut the value of their account in half. The value is now $50,000. What amount are they required to pull out of their portfolio? You guessed it. Still $4,000. That is no longer 4% of their account, it is now 8% of their account. And what kind of return will they need on their depleted account to get it back to the $100,000 mark? It would require a 100% return – twice the 50% loss they incurred, had there not been a withdrawal. But with the $4,000 withdrawal, they now have only $46,000. It will now take a return of nearly 120% to get back to even. The fact of the matter is that George and Donna will likely never get back to where they were before the market downturn, and compounding the matter is the fact that withdrawals not only continue, but the percentage of them will increase and they will owe taxes on every penny they withdraw. Now you understand why it is unwise to use market-based retirement accounts as sources of income during retirement.

The Prudent Man's Rule (A.K.A. The 4% Withdrawal Rule)

So how much can we safely withdraw from our portfolios and make our money last a lifetime *or* two lifetimes in the case of a married couple? There has been much debate surrounding this topic, especially as of late. This rule that was created decades ago by economists stated that retirees at age 65 should be able to withdraw four percent out of their retirement accounts and safely make their assets last a lifetime within a certain probability. This rule was developed at a time when interest rates were high and the stock market was strong. Even in these good times, there was still a chance it would not work out. They utilized probabilities of greater than 90%. We have to admit that is a pretty good probability, right? But what if that 10% chance happens during your retirement years?

Today we live in a different world of low interest rates and a struggling stock market. For this reason, many articles have been published questioning whether the 4% rule is still all that prudent. Maybe it is the two or three percent rule. I make the comparison to taking a flight. If you were to get on an airplane and begin a long flight, then you heard the captain on the loudspeaker say this… "Hello, folks, this is your Captain speaking. I just want to let you know that we have a tremendous amount of in-flight experience, but today there is a 90% chance we land." I bet you would get off the plane and, if the captain said seventy or eighty percent, I know you would! You don't take those kinds of chances with your life. Well, your retirement income is your livelihood and that shouldn't be risked either.

The thing is you don't have to risk it. There are types of products out there today that can guarantee up to eight percent cash flow from your portfolio from the rest of your life without the worry of running out of money or taking part in Reverse Dollar Cost Averaging.

The charts below and on the next page were issued in an article from Vanguard in June of 2009 titled "Revisiting the '4% Spending Rule.'"

LEVERS THAT INFLUENCE SPENDING RATES

	Lower Spending Rate ←——→ Higher Spending Rate	
Time horizon	Longer	Shorter
Asset allocation	More conservative	More aggressive
Portfolio success rates	Higher	Lower

HISTORICAL PORTFOLIO WITHDRAWAL RATES, WHICH RESULTED IN AN 85% SUCCESS RATE

Portfolio	Planning Horizon						
	10 years	15 years	20 years	25 years	30 years	35 years	40 years
Conservative	10.00%	6.75%	5.25%	4.25%	3.75%	3.50%	3.25%
Moderate	10.50%	7.25%	6.00%	5.25%	4.75%	4.50%	4.25%
Aggressive	10.00%	7.00%	6.00%	5.25%	4.75%	4.75%	4.50%

HISTORICAL PORTFOLIO WITHDRAWAL RATES, WHICH RESULTED IN A 75% SUCCESS RATE

Portfolio	Planning Horizon						
	10 years	15 years	20 years	25 years	30 years	35 years	40 years
Conservative	10.50%	7.25%	5.75%	4.50%	4.00%	3.75%	3.50%
Moderate	11.50%	8.50%	6.75%	6.00%	5.25%	5.00%	4.75%
Aggressive	11.00%	8.00%	6.75%	6.00%	5.50%	5.25%	5.00%

Social Security

A discussion regarding retirement income would not be complete without touching on social security. Social Security is another piece of the puzzle that needs to be carefully considered. U.S. News reported that Social Security is the biggest source of retirement income today, with 54% of retirees stating that it is a major source of their retirement income. Furthermore, in 2011, nine out of 10 people age 65 and older received Social Security. For 34% of those individuals, Social Security made up more than 90% of their retirement income. (2012 Guide to Social Security, 40th Edition, Mercer LLC)

Many think Social Security is as straight forward as the notice that is sent out by the Social Security Administration that tells you what amount you are eligible for at different ages. In reality, there is much more to this very important source of retirement income. Many things need to be taken into consideration, including factors such as the potential reduction of benefits, spousal benefits, the taxation of benefits, the effects of divorce, and death. Because of its vital importance to your overall retirement plan, you need to work with someone who can provide you with in-depth knowledge of how it works.

US News reported that Social Security is the biggest source of retirement income today, with 54% of retirees stating that it is a major source of their retirement income.

6%	**Rents and royalties**
8%	**Annuities or insurance**
9%	**Inheritance**
13%	**Savings accounts and CDs**
14%	**Stocks and stock mutual funds**
18%	**Part-time work**
20%	**Home equity**
23%	**Pensions**
45%	**Retirement accounts**
54%	**Social Security**

Frequently Asked Questions

How do I qualify for benefits?

You must be fully insured in order to qualify for Social Security benefits. This means that you must have 40 credits, the equivalent of about 10 years of work. Through 1977, you earned one credit for each calendar quarter in which you had wages or salary of at least $50 in covered employment. This was unfair to many seasonal workers, such as teachers and farmers. So, in 1978 they changed these rules to be based on your annual earnings up to four credits per year. In 2013, one credit is earned for every $1,160 you earn in a year.

How is my benefit calculated?

Your benefit is based on your Primary Insurance Amount (PIA) and your PIA is the amount you receive upon achieving Full Retirement Age (FRA). Your FRA is based on the date you were born. Your average indexed monthly earnings (AIME) are used to calculate your PIA. If you were born after 1929, you use your highest 35 years to calculate your benefits. Your actual earnings are indexed to account for wage changes since the year your earnings were received.

When can I start my benefits?

You can start your benefits as early as age 62. Although depending on your full retirement age, as shown in the chart on the following page, you will receive 20-30% less in benefits as a result of doing so. You will receive your maximum benefit at age 70.

Year of birth	Full retirement age (FRA)	Age 62 benefit reduction
1937 or earlier	65	20.00%
1938	65 and 2 months	20.83%
1939	65 and 4 months	21.67%
1940	65 and 6 months	22.50%
1941	65 and 8 months	23.33%
1942	65 and 10 months	24.17%
1943 – 1954	66	25.00%
1955	66 and 2 months	25.83%
1956	66 and 4 months	26.67%
1957	66 and 6 months	27.50%
1958	66 and 8 months	28.33%
1959	66 and 10 months	29.17%%
1960 and later	67	30.00%

When are my benefits subject to income tax?

Many people are surprised to find their Social Security benefits can be subject to income tax. Whether or not your benefits will be taxed is based on your combined income. That is defined as the sum of the adjusted gross income plus nontaxable interest plus one-half of Social Security benefits. The chart below shows the amount of your Social Security benefit that will be subject to taxation when your combined income crosses certain thresholds.

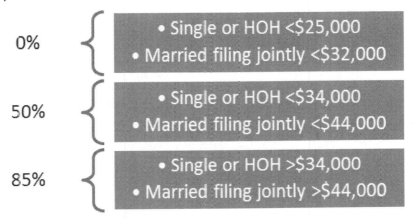

0%
- Single or HOH <$25,000
- Married filing jointly <$32,000

50%
- Single or HOH <$34,000
- Married filing jointly <$44,000

85%
- Single or HOH >$34,000
- Married filing jointly >$44,000

When will my benefits be reduced?

In 2013, if you work into your retirement years and are between age 62 and your full retirement age, you will give up one dollar in benefits for every two dollars you earn over $15,120. In the year of your full retirement age you will give up one dollar for every three dollars you earn over $40,080. There will be no reduction after you have reached your full retirement age.

What benefits are available for my spouse?

You must have been married for at least one year or have a child. If the spouse is at full retirement age the benefit amount is equal to 50% of the PIA of the other spouse. You may elect to receive this spousal benefit prior to FRA, but your benefits will be permanently reduced. Your spouse must first file, before one can draw spousal benefits.

What benefits are available for a divorced spouse?

An ex-spouse can get Social Security benefits based on the other ex-spouse's earnings record, but they must first pass a couple of tests. First, the marriage must have lasted for at least 10 years. Second, he or she must not remarry. Also, if you have been divorced for at least two years and both ex-spouses are at least age 62, the divorced spouse can get benefits even if the ex-spouse is not retired and drawing their benefit.

What happens if I die?

There is a meager death benefit of $255. If you are married, then the largest of the two benefits will continue to the surviving spouse.

The rules regarding Social Security are complicated. You should not only talk to a Social Security representative about your specific situation, but a qualified financial advisor as well. All options and strategies need to be evaluated before you make this very important decision.

(Sources: 2012 Guide to Social Security, 40th Edition, Mercer LLC and the Social Security Administration website)

When **Growth** is Appropriate

Only after you've salted away your emergency fund and secured your future retirement income, is it appropriate that you endeavor to grow your assets with a focus on inflation protection. Ask yourself this: If I have no assets to spend, then what good was my inflation protection? Having your investments before your savings is like learning to ride a bike before you can walk. It's a little dangerous, and it will be difficult to pick yourself up if you crash.

Options abound, however, when it comes to the growth portion of your portfolio during retirement. Some of these options are easy to understand, but the majority are quite complex. Here is a brief explanation of some of the main types of investment options available. (Disclaimer: The definitions provided are simplified and not text book definitions of the investment vehicles referenced. More

traditional definitions can be found at www.finra.org/Investors/
InvestmentChoices/.)

Stocks: Stocks are issued by public corporations
representing an ownership in part of the corporation's assets
and earnings. There are two main types of stocks – common
and preferred. While both have voting rights for
shareholders' meetings and typically issue dividends,
preferred stock carries less risk than common stock, as it has
first priority in the event a company goes bankrupt or is
liquidated and also has first claim on dividends issued.

Options: Options are one of the most difficult investment
vehicles to understand. There are two main types, call
options and put options. Call options create returns only
when the price of a stock increases, while put options create
returns only when the price of a stock decreases. A call
option gives the owner the right to purchase the underlying
stock at a specified price within a set time frame, whereas a
put option gives the owner the right to sell the underlying
stock at a specified price within a set time period. Options are
flexible investment vehicles and can be quite complex, and a
full explanation of their mechanics could fill an entire book.

Mutual Funds: Mutual funds give the opportunity for small
investors to create a diversified portfolio of investments with
relatively low minimums. Mutual funds are operated by
money managers who invest the funds' capital in securities
such as stocks, bonds, money market instruments, and more.

Exchange Traded Funds (ETFs): Exchange traded funds
typically have lower costs than mutual funds, as they are
designed to track a specific index or area of the market.
Because they attempt to track a specific index rather than
outperform the index, the trading costs are minimized to a
large extent. Furthermore the expense ratios are lower than
those of comparable mutual funds, because ETF providers
do not take on the accounting in-house or include 12b-1 fees
related to marketing costs, as mutual funds do. An ETF may

be designed to mimic the returns of the S&P 500, technology stocks, or even the growth of a specific country. Exchange Traded Funds can be actively traded throughout the day, in contrast to a mutual fund that can be sold only at the end of the trading day.

Variable Annuities: Variable annuities typically allow investments in what are referred to as subaccounts; theses subaccounts contain mutual funds. Typically, the primary objective of purchasing a variable annuity is tax deferment. Variable annuities combine the tax-deferred status of an annuity with the open-ended characteristics of market investments. Furthermore, they are often utilized with accompanying guarantees for income or death benefits. These guarantees come with a cost in addition to the base contract fees and expense ratios of the investments selected. Variable annuities are regarded as having very high costs of ownership.

Bonds: Bonds are debt instruments issued by corporations or governments to raise funds for a variety of projects and activities. You typically receive a fixed rate of return for a defined period of time. During that time period, you may be able to liquidate your position, but the price you receive will be determined by market factors such as current interest rates and credit ratings of the company backing the bond. For this reason, they should not be regarded as "liquid" investments. Furthermore, as a result of the inverse relationship between bond prices and interest rates, it can be dangerous to purchase bonds in low-rate environments.

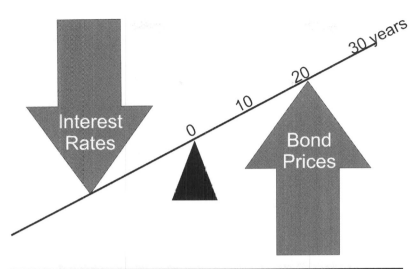

Bond Prices and Interest Rates		
Bond Maturity	*Initial Principle of $1,000 and Yield of 10%**	
	1% Rise in Rates	1% Decline in Rates
Short-Term (2.5 Year Maturity)	$979 -2.1%	$1,022 +2.2%
Intermediate Term (7 Year Maturity)	$952 -4.8%	$1,051 +5.1%
Long Term (20 Year Maturity)	$920 -8.0%	$1,092 +9.2%
*The 10% yield shown is hypothetical and is not intended to show, or project, the performances of any bond or bond fund for any period of time.		

Real Estate Investment Trusts (REITs): REITs may be public or private, meaning they can actively be traded on the major stock exchanges or may have limited or no liquidity. REITs allow smaller investors to participate in areas of the market where they would be typically excluded, such as shopping malls, office buildings, large business loans, etc. These investments typically carry special tax benefits and relatively high yields.

Maybe some of these investments struck you as income vehicles rather than growth vehicles, but remember the word I just used – investments. All of the preceding vehicles are investments. As mentioned earlier, you should never put your required income source at risk. However, once you've taken care of your basic living expenses with savings vehicles backed by a legal reserve system, then maybe you can use these vehicles to create extra income. It would be unwise to move into any of these investment vehicles until your livelihood has been ensured.

The Evolution of Money Management

Now that we've discussed the main types of investment options available for the growth portion of your portfolio, let us discuss how these investments have historically been used. Traditionally, you have probably gone to your broker for assistance in the recommendation of stock, bond, and mutual fund purchases. This broker may have created a balanced/diversified portfolio for you, based on your goals and risk tolerance. You were then scheduled to either rebalance once or twice per year during regular meetings. Your broker may even make recommendations as new opportunities are brought to his or her attention. There is an obvious problem with this mentality that you may have experienced over the last several years. TIME! How much time does your broker really have to manage your investments? And over the lost decade in the early 2000s how well did this management, err I say lack of management, work for your investment portfolio.

I once attended a financial advisory conference where one of the top asset gatherers spoke. I would define an asset gatherer as a financial advisor who gathers large amounts of assets for a broker dealer. This advisor was obviously intelligent and a very hard worker. In the year of this conference, he gathered over $40 million in assets as a single advisor – quite astounding! When asked about his asset management philosophy, he said he invested his client's funds using mutual funds with conservative and balanced approaches. He went on to say that as his mutual fund business grew, he found it necessary to hire someone to manage them. Then he said, "The management of my clients' market based investments is not a full-time job, so I have this person do many other things."

The Purpose Based Retirement

This blew me away! I couldn't believe the management of the riskiest part of his client's portfolio was not a full-time job. This was just two years after 2008. I am sure his clients would be troubled to learn the management of their life savings was "not a full-time job." This was a financial advisor who was conducting two evening seminars a week, working over 60 hours per week, meeting with clients and prospective clients, managing his office team, paying his bills, being a family man, putting on conferences for other advisors, staying physically fit, and trying to continually grow his practice. I'm sure that when his clients came to him to manage their assets, they expected their funds to be actively managed on a full-time basis. However, this is the way 90% of financial advisors work, utilizing mutual funds, mostly strip mall advisors, to carry out their management duties. If this advisor was being completely honest with his clients, I'm sure he would have admitted he doesn't have the time or resources to bring a high level of money management to the table.

I want the person managing my assets to make it their first priority. The sad truth is that most financial advisors simply do not have the time. In my opinion we must change this mentality and I believe the investment world is evolving to allow it to do so.

A brief look back in history shows what changes took place. In 1950, the philosophy most brokers embrace today was adopted. It's often referred to in layman's terms as "buy-and-hold." The buy-and-hold idea was drawn from something called the Modern Portfolio Theory, which was put forward by economist Harry Markowitz in 1952, winning him and his constituents, William F. Sharpe and Merton H. Miller, a Nobel Prize in Economic Sciences. With the stock market volatility experienced in the decade that began in 2000, many cleverly changed the phrase to "buy and hope." According to the Library of Economics and Liberty, the theory looks at "how investment returns can be optimized."

I am sure you, like most investors, had the common sense concept of diversification hammered into your head for years. But Markowitz showed how to measure the risk of various securities and combine them in a portfolio to get the maximum return for a given risk. Here is an explanatory excerpt from the Library of Economics and Liberty on the mechanics of Markowitz's theory:

"Say, for example, shares in Exxon and in General Motors have a high risk and a high return, but one share tends to go up when the other falls. This could happen because when OPEC raises the price of oil (and therefore of gasoline), the prices of oil producers' shares rise and the prices of auto producers' shares fall. Then a portfolio that includes both Exxon and GM shares could earn a high return and have a lower risk than either share alone."

Portfolio managers began using the techniques based on Markowitz's original insight. The technical definition from the Financial Times Lexicon says it like this:

"The theory that an investor can maximize returns by holding a diversified portfolio of assets with different levels of risk. The return from a single asset is less important than how that asset's value moves against overall portfolio values. By looking at the statistical relationship between all the assets in a portfolio, on a risk and return basis, the investor can optimize returns against a chosen level of acceptable risk."

The Encyclopedia of Business, second edition, has this to say:

"Underlying this strategy is the assumption that markets are reasonably efficient, and that any attempt to improve the rate of return from risky securities is not likely to succeed.

This is where the Efficient Market Hypothesis, on which Modern Portfolio Theory is founded, comes into play. According to the online reference site Investopedia.com, the definition of the EMH is:

"An investment theory that states it is impossible to "beat the market" because stock market efficiency causes existing share prices to always incorporate and reflect all relevant information. According to the EMH, stocks always trade at their fair value on stock exchanges, making it impossible for investors to either purchase undervalued stocks or sell stocks for inflated prices. As such, it should be impossible to outperform the overall market through expert stock selection or market timing, and that the only way an investor can possibly obtain higher returns is by purchasing riskier investments."

The development of Modern Portfolio Theory and the Efficient Frontier Hypothesis resulted in the widely used asset management philosophy today referred to as Strategic Asset Allocation, defined by Investopedia as, a portfolio strategy that involves periodically rebalancing the portfolio in order to maintain a long-term goal for asset allocation. As the value of assets changes over time, so the portfolio needs to be adjusted consistently to bring it back to the portfolio's guidelines. This is called rebalancing.

You've probably had your portfolio regularly rebalanced over the years if you've been working with a broker, or saving in your 401(k). Strategic Asset Allocation and these different theories have merits, but they also have downsides. You probably experienced this during what is referred to as the "lost decade," the 10-year period ending in 2010 that saw no gain for the broad U.S. stock market.

Putting aside all of the fancy lingo and definitions of the financial and economic world, this strategy can be summed up by saying we will diversify across the assets that have historically performed well together, and rebalance on a regular basis to retain the same goal allocations.

The World Is Changing

So why is it that our method for investing for growth has to change? Simply put, the markets drastically changed over the last 60 years. The traditional investment philosophy based on Modern Portfolio Theory developed in the 1950's is simply not so modern anymore. Two seemingly small changes were made since those days that forever altered the market's movement.

Employee Reitirement Income Security Act (ERISA)

From 1983 to 2000, the period of time in which the majority of retirees accumulated what they have today, the Dow Jones Industrial Average (DJIA) gained an astounding 1,003.19%. Yes, you heard me correctly. It was the strongest bull market in history. If you invested $100,000 in the stock market in 1983, you would have $1,003,190 just 17 years later. Not a bad return. Obviously many different factors led to the incredible bull run, but to me the one reason that stands out among all others is the introduction of the Revenue Act of 1978, which included a provision that became known as the Internal

Revenue Code (IRC) Sec. 401(k), the section for which these qualified retirement plans are named. With 401(k)s, employees are not taxed on the portion of income they elect to receive as deferred compensation rather than as direct cash payments. The law went into effect on Jan. 1, 1980, and regulations were issued in November 1981. The new provision allowed you to take funds directly from your paycheck, defer taxation on them, and inject them straight into the stock market. From 1979-1982 several companies including Johnson & Johnson, FMC, PepsiCo, JC Penney, Honeywell, Savannah Foods & Industries, Hughes Aircraft Company, and Coates, Herfurth & England, developed 401(k) plan proposals. Many of these retirement programs, in concert with the new law, went into operation in January 1982. Within two years of the regulations going into effect, nearly half of all large firms were either already offering a 401(k) plan for their employees or considering offering one. The Dow Jones Industrial Average at the end of 1982 was 875.00 and the bull run was about to begin. (Data source: Employee Benefit Research Institute)

Prior to the introduction of these Defined Contribution Plans, such as 401 (k)s or 403 (b)s, the majority of retirement benefits came in the form of a pension. These Defined Benefit Pension plans were regulated in a way that limited risk and in turn stock market exposure. Once ERISA was introduced, these plans began to fall to the wayside. According to the Social Security Administration, from 1980 through 2008, the proportion of private wage and salary workers participating in Defined Benefit Pension plans fell from 38% to 20%, a decline of nearly 50%. One of the primary causes of such a shift was the dramatic reduction of risk and liability to the employer. If you have a pension plan today, then consider yourself lucky. As funds began to flow out of Defined Benefit Plans and into Defined Contribution plans the market began to rise. This is what I consider the main contributor to the bull run of the 1980s and 1990s, and what contributed to the slow growth the stock market experienced after that heyday ended in 2000 and will continue to experience for decades to come.

Baby Boomer Tsunami Economics

Nothing quite shaped the demographics of our nation like what has been dubbed the "baby boom" of post-World War II America. Americans born between 1947 and 1964 are "Baby Boomers." When the soldier boys returned home from saving the world for democracy in 1945, they started finding jobs and raising families. A dramatic surge in the birthrate ensued, and it was a generational passing of the torch. This new bunch had not lived through the Great Depression of the 1930s. America was booming and the factories were soon putting out cars with tail fins and miracle appliances such as refrigerators that made ice and microwave ovens. Television was no longer a diversion for the rich; there was one in every living room. The black-and-white world of *Leave it to Beaver* and *Ozzie and Harriett* typified an America that was shedding its conservatism by degrees and swallowing whole all the material goods the country could produce.

Baby Boomers gave us rock and roll and men on the moon. They were the first generation who learned the art of "buy now-pay later." Baby Boomers grew up under the threat of "the bomb" and lived to see the end of the Cold War and the fall of Communism.

The "boom generation" continues to impact the economic landscape. As of January 1, 2011, the first Baby Boomers turned 65. The bobby-soxers of the 1950s and 1960s were ready to retire! According to the U.S. Census Bureau, the first group of 78 million boomers alive today are lining up for Medicare. This phenomenon has been called "The Baby Boomer Tsunami" because boomers are turning 65 at a rate of around 8,000 per day. It is projected that by 2020, 25% of the American workforce will be 55 or older.

Statistics reveal that Baby Boomers control over 80% of personal financial assets and are responsible for more than half of all consumer spending in the nation. They buy 77% of all prescription drugs, 61% of over-the-counter drugs, and are responsible for 80% of all leisure travel. As these Baby Boomers retire, they'll go through the same process as you, looking for the right advisor to protect their assets and create income from their savings. What does this mean? It means that in the future, as Baby Boomers retire and remove money from their savings to fund their living expenses, the inflow of replacement investment dollars will be slower than the outflow.

Americans are having fewer babies. That means there will be fewer workers pumping money into 401(k)s and fewer individual investors contributing to the market.

Lending support to the belief that today's young families are having smaller families is the fact that Americans had fewer babies in 2011 than in any year before, according to Brady Hamilton of the Centers for Disease Control and Prevention. All of this will impact the economic landscape for years to come.

Some of the more apparent obstacles blocking economic growth as this book is written include: the housing crisis, European sovereign debt, the U.S. debt crisis, inflation, trade deficits, high frequency trading, slow GDP growth, China slowing down, natural disasters, and war and terrorist attacks, to name a few. It's no wonder, with all of that over our heads as a nation, that many feel the outlook for future economic growth is bleak.

The great mind of Pimco CEO Bill Gross, who coined the term "The New Normal," believes U.S. economic growth will be stuck averaging less than 2% per year over the next decade. Here is his take on the economic future:

> *"The biblical metaphor of seven years of fat leading to seven years of lean may be quite apropos in the current case with the observation that the developed world's growth binge has been decades in the making. We may need at least a decade for the healing."*

This begs the question, then – "If we are now in a new slow growth economy that could last for another 10 or more years, how are we to invest?"

Dynamic Asset Allocation and Separately Managed Accounts (SMAs)

Industry research has shown that more than 90% of the variation in portfolio return is determined by asset allocation, so its importance cannot be understated. (Source: Brinson Hood Beebower Study) However, there are periods of time where certain assets will outperform others and periods of time where there is enhanced risk that should be hedged. Bringing that level of management to your portfolio may seem impossible. Why is that? Well, let's think about that for a minute… how could any single financial advisor or broker have the time to do all of the research it takes to actively manage your portfolio, constantly seeking new opportunities, sifting through financials, economic trends, and the daily news? That's right. We can't. Let me humbly confess that I don't have the time to actively manage your investment portfolio at the level that it should be managed. But thankfully, there has begun a revolution in money management today that addresses this challenge.

While your advisor may not be able to manage your portfolio at the highest level, he or she may have the ability to seek out what is referred to as a third-party money manager. Using this system is like finding your very own Peter Lynch, widely recognized as one of the most successful money managers of all time as head of the Fidelity Magellan Fund. If you tried to hire Lynch to manage your portfolio in the '80s, he likely would have said you don't have enough money to make it worth his time. That's true of your mutual fund broker today. They will say, if they're honest, "I really don't have time to actively manage your retirement portfolio with individual stocks and bonds, but we can structure a diversified and balanced portfolio of mutual funds and rebalance once or twice a year." A third-party money manager, also called "separately managed accounts," however, can give you your very own investment management team of experts, if you meet investment minimums, which can be as small as $25,000.

This approach is somewhat complex, and can be challenging for retirees and pre-retirees to grasp immediately. Please allow me to drag out the whiteboard and explain the difference between these types of accounts and mutual funds.

A Separately Managed Account, or SMA, is a portfolio of assets under the management of a professional investment firm. In the United States, these firms are usually referred to as Registered Investment Advisors, and they operate under the regulatory auspices of the Investment Advisors Act of 1940 and under the purview of the U.S. Securities and Exchange Commission (SEC). There are also smaller Registered Investment Advisors with assets under $100 million that don't register at a federal level, but with the state securities agency in the state where they have their principal place of business.

One or more portfolio managers are responsible for the day-to-day investment decisions and are supported by a team of analysts, as well as operations personnel and administrative staff. SMAs differ from pooled vehicles like mutual funds in the respect that each portfolio is unique to a single account. In other words, if you set up a separate account with Money Manager X, then Manager X has the discretion to make decisions for this account that may be different from decisions made for other accounts. Say, for example, a manager operates a diversified core equity strategy including 20 stocks. That manager decides to launch a mutual fund containing these stocks and also a separately managed account offering. Assume that, at the outset, the manager invests all portfolios with the same weight – both the mutual fund and the SMAs.

From a client's perspective, the beneficial interests in either vehicle are identical at the outset, but the statements will look different. For the mutual fund client, the position will show up as a single-line entry bearing the mutual fund ticker – most likely a five-letter acronym ending in "X." The value will be the net asset value from the close of business on the statement's effective date. The SMA investor's statement, however, will list each of the equity positions and values separately, and the total value of the account will simply be the aggregate value of each of the positions. From this beginning point, things will begin to diverge. Decisions the manager makes for the mutual fund – including the timing for purchase and sale of shares, dividend reinvestment and distributions – will affect all fund investors in the same way. For SMAs, however, the decisions are at the account level and will therefore vary from one investor to another.

Mass Customization

The high level of customization is one of the main selling points of SMAs, particularly when it comes to individual taxable accounts. Portfolio transactions have expense and tax implications. With managed accounts, investors can feel like they have a greater degree of control over these decisions, and that they are more closely attuned to the objectives and constraints set forth in the investment policy statement.

So what is the price of entry for this extra level of customized attention? There is no single answer for the several thousand managers that make up the SMA universe. As a general rule of thumb, the price of entry starts at $100,000. SMAs targeted to high net worth retail investors tend to set account minimum balances between $100,000 and $5 million. For strategies designed especially for institutional managers, minimum account sizes may range from $10 million to $100 million.

For style-based investors who seek exposure to several different investment styles (e.g., large-cap value, small-cap growth) the price of entry goes up, as there will be a separate SMA, and a separate account minimum, for each style chosen. For example, an investor seeking style-pure exposure in the four corners of the style box – large cap, small cap, value and growth – might need to have at least $400,000 available to implement an SMA-based strategy. Other investors may prefer an all-cap blend (or core) approach that could be found through a single manager.

Fee Structure

With a separately managed account, your costs will come in three main areas:

- **Advisory Fees:** Your advisor will usually charge a flat fee for investing, typically 1% per year.

- **Management Fee:** The manager making investment decisions will also charge a management fee. This management fee is also typically 1% per year.

- **Transaction Cost:** Lastly, you still have transaction cost. Regardless of where your funds are invested, there will be a charge. Many Registered Investment Advisors or Third-Party Money Managers are conducting a large number of transactions and negotiate very low charges at their custodian. These charges may be as low as a penny per share. The difference between an SMA and a mutual fund is these charges will be in black and white on your statement and are usually at cost – the full disclosure your hard-earned assets deserve.

One of the difficulties inherent in making apples-to-apples comparisons among investment offerings is that fee structures vary. This is even trickier for SMAs than for mutual funds. Mutual fund fees are fairly straightforward. The key number is the net expense ratio, including the management fee (for the professional services of the team that runs the fund), miscellaneous ancillary expenses, and a distribution charge called a 12(b)1 fee for certain eligible funds. Many funds also have different types of sales charges. Funds are required to disclose this information in their prospectuses and show explicitly how the fund expenses and sales charges would affect hypothetical returns over different holding periods. Investors can easily obtain these prospectuses from the fund's parent company, either online or through the mail.

Separate accounts do not come with prospectuses. Managers list their basic fee structures in a regulatory filing called a Form ADV Part 2. An investor can obtain this document by contacting the manager or online via the SEC public disclosure page (adviserinfo.sec.gov/IAPD/Content/Search/iapd_Search.aspx). Moreover, the published fee schedule in the ADV Part 2 is not necessarily firm – it is subject to negotiation between the investor (or the investor's financial advisor) and the money manager. Often, it's not a single fee but a scale in which the fee (expressed as a percentage of assets under management) decreases as the asset volume (the amount invested) increases.

The Importance of Due Diligence

Because SMAs do not issue registered prospectuses, investors or their advisors need to rely on other sources for investigating and evaluating the manager. In investor-speak, this is referred to as due diligence. A comprehensive due diligence will elicit sufficiently detailed information regarding all of the following areas:

Performance Data: A manager should be prepared to share performance data (annual and preferably quarterly returns achieved) since the inception of the strategy. The information is contained on a composite – a table showing aggregate performance for all fee-paying accounts in that strategy. A good question to ask here is whether the composite complies with the Global Investment Performance Standards set by the CFA Institute and whether a competent third-party auditor has provided a letter affirming compliance with the standards.

You need to know that they performance numbers you are looking at are **REAL**. Many money managers pop up every year showing you a glowing performance history based on what they *would* have done had their model been around during that time period. Hindsight is 20/20 as they say. I want the person managing my money to have a true track record of what they actually did, not what they would have done.

Philosophy and Approach: Each manager has a unique investment philosophy and way of going about applying that philosophy to an investment approach. You'll want to know whether the manager has a more active or passive style, a top-down or bottom-up approach, how he or she manages alpha and beta risk, the strategy's performance benchmark and other similar information.

Investment Process: Find out who makes the decisions and how those decisions get carried out; the roles and responsibilities of portfolio managers, analysts, support staff, and others; who comprises the investment committee and how often it meets; and the sell discipline and other key aspects of the process.

Operations: Some managers have extensive in-house trading platforms, while others outsource all non-core functions to third-party providers like Schwab or Fidelity. You also need to understand transaction expenses and how they can affect your bottom line. Another useful area of information here is client and account services. Among other things, here you can find out about net client activity – how many new clients did the firm originate and how many left over a defined time period? What were the circumstances surrounding those who left?

Organization and Compensation: How the firm is organized and how it pays its professionals – especially the managers whose reputations and track records are the big draw – is an extremely important area to cover. Understand the calculations behind incentive compensation. Are the manager's incentives aligned with those of the investor? This is a must.

Compliance History: Red flags include prominent infractions with the SEC or other regulatory bodies, fines or penalties levied and lawsuits or other adverse legal situations. The SEC considers separate account managers to be investment advisors subject to the provisions of the Investment Advisors Act of 1940. Much of this information can be obtained from the manager's Form ADV Parts 1 and 2 (with Part 2 having more of the details on strategy, approach, fees, and biographical information on the principal team members). Performance data should be available directly from the manager, either online or through personal contact with a manager representative. The representative should also be able to coordinate phone or in-person meetings with key team members, and direct your questions appropriately on compliance and other issues.

Why Separately Managed Accounts?

Separately Managed Accounts (SMAs) provide a massive amount of efficiency to your financial life. Mutual funds can be a great starting point for beginning investors, but once you have accumulated significant assets you have to assess much more efficient options. While mutual funds can provide you access to professional money management and diversification, they can also provide many additional benefits. These benefits include potentially lowering overall expenses, tax efficiency, customization, control over the maturity of your bond portfolio, and most importantly the *TRANSPARENCY* your hard earned dollar deserves.

Income Driven Investing

As I said in an earlier chapter, because of my conservative approach, I have sometimes been called the "dinosaur in the corner of your portfolio." Jim Cramer would tell me that, with my time frame of over 20 years on my retirement assets, I should be investing in growth stocks. But if we're in for an extended period of slow growth, why would I want to do this? I believe that investing for growth has the potential to yield sub-par returns for the next 10 or 20 years. Instead of investing for growth, I choose to invest for income. And if I can create 5% to 6% in the form of dividends from a relatively conservative portfolio, I'll be able to create decent returns. That way, if we do experience some growth, my returns can only improve.

The bottom line is this: Markets have evolved and so must our strategies. The traditional buy-and-hold money management philosophy may no longer be the best way to go. Strategic Asset Allocation may be a thing of the past and a higher level of money management may be necessary in this new age of high volatility and slow growth.

Estate Planning Takes a Village

Many think of estate planning as spoiling the next generation by giving them money they didn't necessarily work for, but it is much more complex than that. Estate planning is the collection of preparatory tasks that serve to manage an individual's incapacitation or death, including bequest of assets to heirs and the settlement of estate taxes. Some of the major tasks include creating a will, limiting estate taxes through the use of trust accounts, establishing a guardian for living dependents, naming an executor of the estate to oversee the terms of the will, establishing beneficiaries, setting up funeral arrangements, annual gifting techniques, addressing potential long-term care needs, and establishing durable power of attorney (POA) to direct other assets and investments.

Estate planning is an ongoing process and should be started as soon as possible. Even if you have minimal assets, an advanced medical directive should be in place, the sooner the better. An advanced medical directive is designed to outline a person's wishes and preferences in regard to medical treatments and interventions. Even if you have no assets, being incapacitated indefinitely on life support may not be what you would wish to happen. You should always seek the advice of an attorney when establishing your estate plan, but you should involve your financial advisor to ensure that your personal wishes and your financial goals are aligned. Each professional involved in the estate planning process brings his or her own level of expertise to the table on behalf of the client. You will find you need each of them working in concert to ensure a successful plan. The attorney, the CPA, and the CFP © are valuable players on this team.

The references to estate planning are for informational purposes only and are not intended to provide legal advice nor serve as the basis for any financial decisions. Be sure to speak with a qualified legal professional before making any decisions regarding your personal situation.

Avoiding the IRA Tax Bomb

As I am writing this, tax rates are not all that devastating considering what they have been historically. The highest marginal tax rate in history was 94% during World War II. Consider what would happen to your IRA if you were to pass it on to your heirs at a time when taxes were that high. Let's say you have a $500,000 IRA and your two children are your only beneficiaries. If you were to die, Uncle Sam would be the first to take a chunk out of your life savings. The government would get as much as $400,000 of your hard earned cash, while your two children split the remaining $100,000. Of course, this is if your children decide to take your IRA in a lump sum to go buy their new hot tubs and sports cars. But you do have options to ensure this doesn't happen. In this chapter, we will discuss strategies to disinherit Uncle Sam and maximize the amount of cash you pass onto your heirs. It's called IRA Optimization.

Many of the clients with whom I worked over the years, from all manner of economic backgrounds – multi-millionaire bankers to blue collar savers – have IRAs they'll never spend. If you know you'll never need your IRA, why not employ a strategy that can maximize the value of your IRA while minimizing the taxes that will ultimately be paid by your beneficiaries?

In most instances, you pay lower taxes during retirement than you paid during your working years. Your income may consist of mostly Social Security with minimal taxable income sprinkled in. When you turn 70½, the IRS forces you to begin taking distributions from your IRA, called Required Minimum Distributions (RMDs). You are required to make these withdrawals whether or not you need the income. Let's use a real life example, with some facts changed, of course, to mask the identity of our client.

In 2012, we met Gary and Susan. Gary was a banker from New York City who decided to retire with a pension of $30,000 per year. The couple would also have combined Social Security benefits of $25,000 per year. In addition, Gary took dividend income from his $500,000 non-qualified, or after-tax, portfolio for a little extra spending money. Rounding out their financial picture was Gary's 401(k), which he rolled over into an IRA worth another $500,000. Gary recently turned 70½ and was forced to begin taking his RMDs. This distribution is approximately $20,000 per year. Gary obviously doesn't need the income. In fact, he is a bit irked that he is forced to take the distribution and pay taxes on it. But those are the rules. Gary paid no taxes on the money while it was growing in the 401(k), nor did he pay taxes on the money while it was growing inside the IRA. Gary's IRA is invested where it earns a fixed 5% return per year. When each RMD comes out, he pays taxes on it. He is in a 20% tax bracket. He then reinvests the RMD, earning the same 5% fixed interest. By the time he and his wife reach age 85, their life expectancy according to the government, the account will be worth much less than it otherwise would have been had he not been required to go through the motions of withdrawing it, paying taxes on the withdrawal, and then reinvesting it.

Gary and Susan are most concerned about their daughter, Carey, a single mother of two. They want to make sure she is left with enough money to take care of herself and their grandchildren. When Carey inherits that IRA along with the non-qualified funds that have been reinvested, she will be in the highest tax bracket possible. Inheriting a lump sum has a way of doing that. Uncle Sam will get at least 40% of Carey's inheritance, a fact that irks Gary even more. But what other option do Gary and Susan have?

Drum roll, please.

Gary and Susan could deposit their IRA into a hybrid annuity that guarantees they can distribute $34,000 per year for the rest of their lives. They can pay their taxes as they go and use the remaining funds to create a $1.2 million dollar *tax-free* account for their daughter, Carey.

It is entirely possible to leverage these unneeded **IRA** distributions to purchase life insurance, but not just any life insurance. They may use it to purchase a Guaranteed Universal Life Insurance policy, basically a term to 120 years of age. This life insurance policy will also be leveraged by the fact that we make it a "second-to-die" policy, which will increase the death benefit by 25-35% over what it would be if we were insuring a single life. Now we have guaranteed that their **IRA** will more than double in value, regardless of what the stock market does.

When Gary and Susan die, their daughter will inherit both the remaining funds in their taxable **IRA**, and the tax-free funds in their Guaranteed Universal Life Insurance. Gary and Susan are no longer irked.

At age 85, their joint life expectancy, their daughter is guaranteed to receive $1.2 million – more than double the value of their **IRA** without market risk.

(Disclaimer: The previous example may not be representative of your personal experience. Furthermore, Gary and Susan are fictitious beings and are here to provide the reader with a clearer picture of a financial concept.)

Stretching an IRA

Another option that has gained in popularity over the last decade is something called a stretch **IRA**. A stretch **IRA** allows you to potentially leave behind a legacy that will last for generations to come.

This is in stark contrast to leaving behind a TAX BOMB that could be washed away in a matter of years. Let us take an example using Jerry, age 65, his son, Tim, at age 40, and his granddaughter, Lucy, age 10. Jerry was widowed at age 60 and is very wealthy. Jerry's largest liquid asset, his $500,000 **IRA**, is also set to take the largest tax hit when he passes. Currently the primary beneficiary to Jerry's **IRA** is his son Tim. We advise Jerry to consider naming Lucy as the beneficiary.

Tim's life expectancy is 43.6 years, while Lucy's is 72.8 years. We ask Jerry to assume something tragically happens to him in 2013. If Tim is the beneficiary, his first required distribution is December 31st of 2014 and will be 2.29% of the **IRA** balance or $11,250. (100 divided by a life expectancy of 43.6 years is 2.29%.) However, if Lucy is the beneficiary, the required distribution amount is $6,850, $4,400 less than the distribution required to be paid to Tim. This strategy leaves more money to continue enjoying the benefits of tax deferral, effectively "stretching" the IRA.

Let's take a more likely example and assume that Jerry lives to age 80, 15 more years. The diagram on the next page compares the use of Tim's life expectancy to Lucy's.

Scenario	Tim	Lucy
Distribution to each beneficiary for first year after death of Jerry (2028)	$30,748	$16,841
Cumulative distributions to each beneficiary over that person's life expectancy (2056 for Tim and 2080 for Lucy)	$2,910,456	$9,224,336

In 2028, Lucy as beneficiary is taking out almost 50% less than Tim is required to withdraw. This feeds the cumulative benefit and results in the total payouts to Lucy being almost triple of those that would be made to Tim.

If you decide you want to pursue this strategy, there are certain things that need to be taken into consideration. First off, your beneficiaries have to be on board with the plan. There is nothing stopping them from taking a lump sum if they so wish. You may say, my kids wouldn't do something that silly, but the majority of IRA beneficiaries take the money and run resulting in the detriment of any long-term tax deferral benefits. The money may also be vulnerable to divorce settlements or creditors, and any money withdrawn will lose the inherent protections of the IRA. It may be more prudent to name a trust as the beneficiary of your IRA rather than an individual. A trust can offer important benefits such as:

- There are important estate tax planning benefits with potentially huge tax savings.
- Appropriately structured assets in a trust are not attachable by creditors nor are they marital property of the beneficiary.
- Control of assets otherwise payable to a minor or to a person who is incompetent or who cannot handle his or her finances.
- The trust solves the problem of a successor beneficiary where the initial trust beneficiary dies before complete distribution of an inherited IRA account.
- Property in a trust can avoid probate at the death of a beneficiary.

While a simple trust has its merits, it can also have its downfalls when it comes to distribution rules for IRAs. The IRS requires that the required minimum distribution for the IRA in a trust be distributed based on the age of the oldest beneficiary. This dramatically reduces the tax benefits attempting to be accomplished by "stretching" the IRA. Enter IRS Private Letter Ruling 200537044 in 2006, approving an "IRA Trust." Using this new strategy, at the death of the trust owner the trust will divide into smaller "subtrusts," for each beneficiary. This allows the "stretching" of the IRA to continue, while retaining the important benefits of a trust as described previously. Combining this strategy with life insurance can create multiple levels of benefits that can last for generations to come.

Thinking Outside the Box with Long-Term Care Insurance

I hear many colorful expressions from retirees about how they plan to avoid the nursing home.

"I have instructed my wife to just take me into the back yard and use my .22," joked one man. I told him that, while that may seem to be a reasonable solution to him, his lovely wife may not be too wild about spending her remaining years in prison.

"We've taken care of our kids, so now it's their turn," said another couple. But what if your kids can't afford to take care of you? Or what if they would like to care for you, but your failing health makes it mandatory you receive a level of professional medical care they are incapable of providing? Not many adult children, even if they're willing, can bear the expense of caring for an aging parent while continuing to maintain their own household, pay for their children's college education, and save for their own retirement.

Some say they will just go on Medicaid and let the government take care of them. I've heard this from people who have considerable assets. The plan is to consult with an attorney and simply rearrange those assets in order to qualify for Medicaid. Everything is hunky-dory, right? Now your assets are safe and your care is paid for by the state. There is the quality of care issue to be considered. What kind of care do you think Medicaid will provide? Are you going to get the private apartment room you envision and the attentive nurse you deserve to take care of you? Not likely. Picture getting a shared room with only a flimsy curtain between you and the high school classmate you never got along with. Picture the nurse who failed her board exams three times before she passed and can't hit a vein for the life of her. Even if you're able to qualify for Medicaid and save your assets from the home, are you still receiving the care you deserve? Probably not.

So what are the alternatives? What are the ways you can protect yourself from these potential devastating fates? Are you thinking long-term care insurance? If you're a retiree or soon to be retired, then you've probably been pitched long-term care insurance more often than you've received telemarketing calls about hearing aids. Don't get me wrong. Long-term care insurance can be a great asset. But you must purchase it at the right time. The older you are, the more it costs. Unfortunately, most people wait too long. Either their age catches up with them or they develop health issues that prevent them from qualifying for the insurance. Age 60 is really the "sweet spot" for long-term care insurance premiums. After that, premiums can skyrocket.

The Baby Boom generation has been less than enthusiastic about traditional LTC insurance, mainly because of the "use-it-or-lose-it" aspect. When my father was 62, I looked into long-term care insurance for him. The premium for total asset protection would have been around $5,000 per year. This meant that we could purchase a long-term care policy and pay $5,000 per year for potentially the rest of his life and never use the policy. Let's say Dad never used the insurance. What happens to all of the money we paid in premiums? Would it be returned with interest? Dream on. It wouldn't be returned at all. It's like car insurance or fire insurance (only much more expensive). All of the money we paid in premiums would go straight to the insurance carrier. You can see why some people blanch when they do the math on this one. What if you contemplate spending $5,000 per year (a number that can increase, by the way, at the discretion of the insurance company) at age 62 and you are relatively healthy? Is there a possibility you'll live another 30 years? Of course! It is in fact quite probable if you're healthy. Figure up what $150,000 is at 5% compounded interest.

What our family did instead was purchase a life insurance policy that carries what is called a "linked benefit." Instead of paying $5,000 per year for something we may or may not ever use, we could pay that cash into a life insurance policy with a $500,000 death benefit – and with this important provision: **we could use these funds for long-term care if needed!** At least this way we knew the money paid into the policy would be returned with interest later in life. This isn't the answer for everyone. Some may have physical ailments that prevent them from qualifying for life insurance or long-term care insurance.

Thinking Outside the Box

About 10 years ago the insurance industry, seeing that traditional long-term care policies weren't exactly flying off the shelves, went to work designing a different approach. Kudos to them for thinking outside the box. What does that expression mean? It means to think independently of tradition. Find a new way. Ditch conventional thinking and invent an unexpected solution. Think fresh, not stale. I could go on and on, but you get the point. One of the greatest assets a holistic planner can possess is the capacity to think outside the box. Pushing the limits of our creativity enables us to see solutions we might not otherwise catch sight of. We can illustrate it with this simple puzzle. Connect the dots in the square shown here by drawing no more than four continuous straight lines. (The solution is on the next page.)

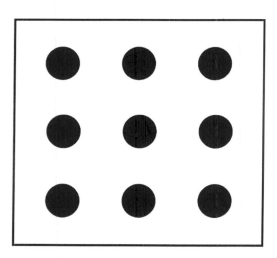

If you notice, we said nothing about going outside the box. Were you able to think outside the box?

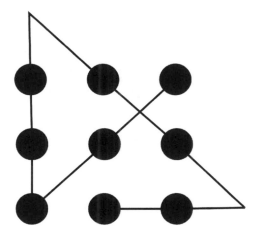

The insurance industry, thinking outside the box, came up with a product they call the "combo." It is called that because it combines an annuity with long-term care coverage. The first ingredient of the combo is a regular fixed annuity that gives you a guaranteed minimum return of approximately 3% with the ability to participate in the upside of the market up to a certain amount (I've seen caps as high as 14% per year.) The second piece is long-term care coverage that works like this: Say you purchased a $100,000 combo. It could potentially pay long-term care benefits of up to $300,000, with your initial $100,000 used up first. That's a general example. There are three or four versions of this product on the market. The underwriting for these programs, if required, is typically much more liberal than what is required by traditional long-term care insurance. If you never need the long-term care benefits, then pass the $100,000, as well as the gains, on to your loved ones when you die.

The life insurance combo works on the same principle but the moving parts function differently. The point is that alternatives to traditional LTC insurance do exist. They are slowly catching on. Insurance companies have done a good job designing them, but, in my opinion, a poor job marketing them because few people know they exist.

Another type of linked benefit option is available with what are called "hybrid annuities," which is an insurance nickname for a Fixed Index Annuity with an income rider. I've incorporated FIAs with income riders more and more in my practice in recent years because they provide the solution to many problems associated with retirement. (More on this later.) Some versions of this type of annuity can guarantee you a lifetime income stream that increases every year. It acts like a secondary pension to supplement Social Security or any other source of income you have available in retirement. Some of these products carry a provision that doubles the income if the income beneficiary is in a nursing home or needs home health care. These products require no underwriting and are a good fit for retirees who want long-term care benefits but do not want to be saddled with the high premium costs associated with traditional LTC insurance.

Casey Weade

Chapter Five

Watch Out For Hidden Investment Fees!

The more hidden the venom, the more dangerous it is.

~ Marguerite De Valois

I'm often asked, "What is your number one frustration with the financial industry?" My always-consistent answer is, "Hidden fees!" Hidden fees are abundant in the financial industry, and there are a couple of products that consistently illustrate this fact – mutual funds and variable annuities. Exercise caution if your potential retirement advisor is enthusiastically pushing these products.

Many individuals believe their advisor only makes money when something is bought or sold. In stark contrast, mutual funds often contain ongoing fees that are not consistently, adequately disclosed in addition to those that are disclosed in the prospectus for the fund. The fees inside a mutual fund are:

Loads: There are many different classes of mutual funds with different types of loads or charges. There are typically three main types of mutual fund classes:

A Shares contain a front load that is charged upon your initial investment, reducing your initial deposit typically around 5%. These shares have lower expense ratios and may allow discounts for larger deposits.

B Shares have back-end loads, or contingent deferred sales charges. There are no upfront fees, you have a sales charge that goes down over time, and usually convert to A shares after a certain period of time (beneficial because A shares typically have a lower annual expense ratio).

C Shares have no upfront charges as this is captured in the form of higher on-going expenses, but may have a back-end load of around 1% that is usually removed after the fund has been held for one year.

Expense Ratios: Besides loads, this is the only cost many retirees and pre-retirees are aware of. The expense ratio is used to pay distribution costs, management fees, and marketing costs. According to a 2009 study of thousands of U.S. equity mutual funds the average trading costs is 1.44% as a direct cost to investors. (The Hidden Costs of Mutual Funds, Wall Street Journal, 3/1/2010)

Transaction Costs: The costs I have described thus far are the costs disclosed to you as an investor, but that isn't the real bottom line. Other costs are related to the buying and selling of securities within the portfolio. A March 2010 *Wall Street Journal* Article entitled "The Hidden Costs of Mutual Funds," stated, "…those expenses can make a fund two or three times as costly as advertised." The article continued, "A study updated last year (2009) of thousands of U.S.-stock funds put the average trading costs at 1.44% of total assets, with an average of 0.14% in the bottom quintile and 2.96% in the top." The most astounding fact is they are not required to disclose these costs to the investor.

Tax Costs: Tax costs are an often overlooked risk of purchasing mutual funds, especially in non-qualified accounts (non-IRA, 401(k), 403(b), 457, and other tax-deferred accounts). When purchasing a mutual fund you may end up paying taxes on the appreciation of assets in which you never participated. You may experience this if you purchased a mutual fund in the middle of a year such as 2008. In that year, many securities were sold off at substantial gains mid-year, while the fund subsequently lost value through the remainder of the year. Even though you didn't benefit from the gains of investments sold prior to or during the period of time you held the mutual fund, they would still be taxable to you. Had you held the investments inside the mutual fund individually you would have had control over your gains and losses. A Separately Managed Account (SMA) is composed of individual securities with an individual cost basis, this gives you control over the amount and timing of gains and losses. This can reduce the overall tax drag on your portfolio.

Soft Dollar Costs: One of the most difficult mutual fund expenses to uncover is soft dollar costs. Many times mutual fund managers are provided software, education, research, and/or other services by brokerage firms. In exchange for these benefits, the brokerage house may charge a premium for trades. A study conducted by Stephen M. Horan, head of professional education content for CFA (Certified Financial Analysts) Institute, estimated that soft dollar brokerage commissions may total $1 billion annually, or up to 40% of all equity trading costs.

Lackluster Performance: It has been no mystery that the majority of mutual funds have had difficulty providing above average returns or beating the market. US News and World Report stated in a 2012 article titled "Index Funds Still Beat Most Managers" that "In mid-2012 73.24% of active domestic stock mutual funds were unable to beat the benchmark S&P 1500 composite index over the trailing three-year period." I think that this number could be even higher. This is because the statistics commonly quoted by the mutual fund industry utilize a sample of mutual funds that are still active that year. Each year hundreds of mutual funds close their doors and either cash is returned to investors or funds are merged together most often as a result of poor performance. When a fund closes it is no longer included in the studies. Furthermore, one main cause for this underperformance is the significant amount of cash many mutual funds hold on hand. They need to have cash on hand at all times for end of the day redemption requests. They also are constantly receiving new money contributions and there is a delay before this money is allocated to purchase securities. This works against shareholders as that cash earns virtually no interest or dividends in a low interest rate environment. Holding your own Separately Managed Account (SMA) would eliminate this issue as the only person ever needing cash or contributing to your account is YOU!

Advisory Fees: In addition to the internal cost of owning a mutual fund, you may be paying a management fee to your advisor. This fee can range anywhere from .25% up to 2.5%. Most investors believe this is the only fee they are charged. Our analysis shows it can be two or three times more costly. These are just a few of the reasons I regularly recommend Separately Managed Accounts to my clients as a mutual fund alternative. There is complete transparency, no loads or soft dollar costs, and more efficient taxation.

Some Annuities Have Hidden Fees

The second group of products where hidden fees are most abundant are annuities, particularly variable annuities. There are as many different types of annuities today as there are models of automobiles and flavors of ice cream. These vehicles or products can be your own best friend or worst enemy during your retirement years. It is important you understand the difference between them and for what purpose they are best utlized.

Immediate Annuities – Immediate annuities are what most people think of when they hear the word "annuity." This type of annuity can be likened to a pension or Social Security. In most cases you first deposit a lump sum and in return you receive a guaranteed lifetime income. This guaranteed income is referred to as annuitization, or, as I like to refer to it – *annuicide*. I call it that because you are locked into this account at a specific rate for a lifetime with no flexibility. In a low interest rate environment this is very dangerous. NEVER lose control of your dollars! Immediate annuities usually have some of the following options:

Single life: A regular payment is guaranteed for the remainder of your life. If you pass away, nothing is left for your beneficiaries.

Life and Period Certain: This is a guarantee that the insurance company will issue a minimum number of payments, to either you or your named beneficiary, whether you are alive or not. This may be for a period of five, 10, or 20 years. After this period of time, you'll continue to receive payments, but if you were to die, there will be nothing left for your beneficiaries.

Joint and Survivor: A guarantee that you will receive payments for your lifetime and the lifetime of your spouse; however, if you both pass away, there is no benefit to your beneficiaries.

Fixed Annuities – A fixed annuity is one of the most straightforward annuity contracts you can hold. It pays you a fixed rate of interest for a fixed period of time, during which you will usually have limited liquidity (typically 10% of your account value).

There will be penalties for early withdrawal. At the end of this period, you receive a lump sum payout, or you may have the option to annuitize over a specified period or a lifetime. A fixed annuity typically pays a slightly higher rate of interest than a bank CD, which is why I think of them as CDs on steroids. The primary reason they are able to provide higher rates of return is the higher surrender charge that would be incurred in the case of full withdrawal. Whereas a CD typically has a penalty of six months interest, a fixed annuity may have a penalty that results in a loss of principal. Furthermore, a CD is backed by the FDIC, while a fixed annuity is backed by the claims paying ability of the issuing insurance company and the state guarantee association up to the state's respective maximum benefit.

Fixed Index Annuities – Fixed Indexed annuities were introduced in the late 1990s and early 2000s. A fixed indexed annuity will tie your rate of return to the performance of a certain market index, such as the S&P 500, DJIA, or maybe even the price of gold, or sometimes a combination of indices. Your principal is still guaranteed by the insurance company, as in the case of the traditional fixed annuity. The difference is that your rate of return fluctuates year to year based on the index to which your annuity is tied. Many advisors have used deceptive sales tactics when selling these products, asserting that with FIAs you get "the upside of the market with none of the downside." While this statement is partially correct, one element is commonly left out – caps and participation rates. The return you receive from year to year is limited by the insurance company. In the late '90s and early 2000s, it was common to find caps of 10% to 15 Studies have found that a cap of 13.5% on the S&P 500 would have averaged 7.48%, versus 6.45% for the S&P 500 over any given 10-year period from 1928 to 2001. Wouldn't you have rather achieved a higher rate of return than the market **and** enjoyed the reduced stress of avoiding any negative years? But as I write this, caps dropped significantly along with interest rates. Annual caps today are regularly found at 2% or 3%, but they can be much higher. Whenever purchasing a product such as this ensure you are shown all of your options and that means working with an **INDEPENDENT** financial advisor.

As with the fixed annuity, strings are attached to these accounts that you need to be aware of. For one, your money is tied up for a certain period of time with limited liquidity (typically 10% of your account value). After this period is up, you can take the lump sum value of your investment, or you may be able to annuitize this value similar to the way you can an immediate annuity.

Hybrid Annuities – The latest development in the fixed annuity market was the introduction of Hybrid Annuities. Prior to these annuities, if you wanted to receive a guaranteed lifetime income, you had to annuitize a fixed annuity. In contrast, a hybrid annuity is similar to a fixed indexed annuity, but it allows you the option of adding a Guarantee Lifetime Withdrawal Benefit. The GLWB does just what the name implies. It guarantees you an income you can't outlive, regardless of the performance of the basic account. The account may also be set up so the GLWB covers the life of the spouse, as well. Triggering your lifetime income benefits is not the same as annuitizing the contract. These products typically give the investor the flexibility to stop and start the lifetime income benefits and to walk away with the remaining funds in their annuity. Should the annuitant die, the account balance of the contract passes on to heirs typically with interest.

Variable Annuities – Now we have arrived at my true number one daily frustration. Variable annuities have gained in popularity over the last decade, mainly because of the promises that seem to have been made about them by those who market them. Variable annuities are often sold as a product that will give you all of the upside in the market, with guarantees of future income, or death benefits. It sounds like the perfect product, right? Wrong. There is no "magic silver bullet" in the financial world, folks. In return for all of these apparent benefits, you pay dearly. According to AnnyityFYI.com, a website that explores the workings of various retirement concepts and strategies, these fees include:

- o Mortality & Expense Charges (M&E Fees): The industry average is 1.25%.
- o Administration Fee: Industry average is .15%
- o Living Benefit (Income or Return of Premium Benefit): Industry average is 1.10%. These income benefits are

typically watered down versus those available in fixed types of annuities. With variable annuities, you may be able to get a 3% to 4% guaranteed withdrawal rate, but you may be able to obtain a 6% to 8% withdrawal rate with an annuity created specifically for that purpose.

○ Death Benefit Fee: The average Death Benefit Fee is .4%. The death benefit always sounds like such a great deal until you take a closer look. It is taxable! If you're going to pay for a death benefit, buy life insurance – it's tax-free! I've seen account values of $100,000 with a death benefit of $170,000, and individuals feeling as if they are stuck with it for the rest of their lives. But what really happens when they die is that the $70,000 gain is taxable, meaning the beneficiaries inherit $140,000 to $150,000. On the other hand, we could position the $100,000 into a life insurance policy that would create a $225,000 tax-free death benefit. It is all about determining the purpose of your assets and positioning in the most efficient way to accomplish your goals.

○ Mutual Fund Costs: What is often overlooked is that you are investing in mutual funds. As previously discussed, all mutual funds have fees with an expense ratio averaging 1.4%. The inclusion of transaction costs could make these charges two or three times as costly. Add all of these fees together and you could be paying an average of 6%. I have personally reviewed accounts with fees over 7%! With these fees, you can see how any growth in your actual mutual fund account can be quickly watered down. You could potentially be locked into the living or death benefit for the rest of your life, especially if we were to experience a down market. If you're going to invest in the market, do it with as little cost as possible. Why pay an extra 3% or 4% for the annuity shell when your growth is just getting watered down?

○ Surrender Charges: These fees come into play only if you withdraw funds from your variable annuity and typically start around 6% and decrease every year. The average maximum fee according to Morningstar is 5.94%.

It is all about creating specific purposes for your different assets and eliminating inefficiencies. In my opinion, annuities should only be used for limited circumstances. They are not growth vehicles, they are not liquidity vehicles, and they are certainly not the silver bullet solution to your retirement plan. If your potential retirement advisor believes they are, you may want to question his or her motives, and at the very least seek a second opinion. Annuities are great savings and income vehicles they are not investments. They can give you better rates of return than CDs at the bank and secure a high level of retirement income. Never forget to use these vehicles for the purpose they were created this will help unleash the true power of your investable assets.

Bond Mark-Ups

Hidden fees can also be found in bond transactions. According to an article entitled "You May Be Paying Hundreds in Hidden Bond Fees," published in November 2009 by CBS MoneyWatch, banking giant Morgan Stanley was fined $90,000 and ordered to make restitution of more than $40,000 due to charges of abusive trading practices related to corporate and municipal bond trades. "This serves as another illustration of some of the dangers of buying bonds through broker-dealers," the article stated. Pointing out that firms can change the price of bonds as they see fit, the MoneyWatch article continued:

> *Unfortunately, the Municipal Securities Rulemaking Board (MSRB) provides almost no guidelines as to a limit on the amount a broker-dealer can mark up or down the price of a bond. The only guidance is what is known as Rule G-18. It requires that brokers trade at prices that are "fair and reasonable in relation to prevailing market conditions." In Morgan Stanley's case, two municipal bond transactions were marked up 7.41 percent and 6.98 percent, and one was marked down 22.98 percent.*

I find that most investors don't realize the only required disclosure when buying bonds is the transaction fee. They assume it is the only cost they will incur. I like to look at the paperwork when interviewing prospective clients who entered into bond transactions. Sometimes they're shocked to find out the spread they were led to believe would be 1% turned out to be much higher. Usually when a fee is not disclosed to the buyer, it's a good indication the seller knows the fee is unfair and not in the client's best interest. If you're working with a fee-based advisor, your goals and their goals will be aligned, since the higher the cost of purchasing the bond, the lower the ultimate portfolio value; the lower the portfolio value, the lower their earnings will be. If your potential advisor is paid a commission and held to suitability standard versus a fiduciary standard, there is an inherent risk of bias. Instead of having a middleman, the broker-dealer, many institutional fiduciary advisors have the capability of going directly to the wholesaler and eliminating the additional cost of the middleman. Large institutional advisors may be buying large blocks at a time for multiple client accounts. This "buying power" allows you to get a better price than if you were to buy smaller lots on your own.

Since there is no legal requirement that markups or markdowns be disclosed to investors, it is important to do your research. (http://www.forbes.com/2009/02/26/munis-spreads-markups-personal-finance_investing_ideas_bond_brokers.html) There are very few ways you can determine the markups and markdowns that you receive, other than subscribing to costly financial information services, such as Bloomberg. You may obtain information free of charge by accessing the websites that are administered by the Financial Industry Regulatory Authority (FINRA) and the Municipal Securities Rulemaking Board (MSRB). These sources will help you determine the bond prices in general and what price is being paid for your specific bond. The difference between this price and the

price you pay your broker is the "markup." Another example of how substantial these markups can be is the big global bank Citigroup. Joe Light in his Wall Street Journal blog of March 19, 2012, reported that the banking giant was fined over $600,000 for charging excessive markups on corporate and agency bonds. Light quoted FINRA as stating that Citi International Financial Services, a subsidiary of Citigroup, charged markups or markdowns of 2.73% to more than 10% – which was in excess of the spread they should have charged, given market conditions.

Markups for retail investors are typically 1% to 2%. If you're working with an institutional fee-based firm you may have no mark-up, but you will have an ongoing annual fee of .10% to 1%. Generally, the more actively your manager works with your bond portfolio, the higher the fee. Thomas Doe, Chief Executive Officer of Municipal Market Advisors, a Concord, Massachusetts-based research firm, stated that firms selling to customers mark up the price an average of $5 to $10, or .50% to 1%. Do your due diligence and know what you're getting.

In closing, it is vitally important that you understand how valuable it is to avoid hidden fees and charges in your retirement plan. You must keep as many of your hard earned dollars in your account working for you as possible. This chart illustrates the growth of $100,000 at 7% per year with a one, two and three percent annual cost.

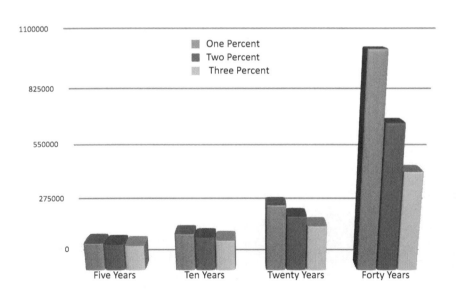

Chapter Six

Is My Money Safe?

*We are all travelers in the wilderness of this world, and the best we can find in
our travels is an honest friend.*

~ *Robert Louis Stevenson*

The phrase "Ponzi scheme" dominated more than one headline
when the turbulent aftermath of the 2008 market crash caused the
collapse of the house-of-cards investment fraud engineered by the
now infamous Bernie Madoff. He is currently serving a 150-year
prison sentence for bilking innocent victims out of billions of dollars.

Charles Ponzi was an Italian con artist who rose to infamy in the
early 1920s after he perfected the game of promising clients
unreasonably high returns over a short period of time; the early
investors received their returns on the backs of later investors who
would eventually be left holding the bag. If you ask me,
lexicographers should rename such investment chicanery "Madoff
schemes," since Madoff's crime makes Ponzi's look like shoplifting by
comparison.

Post Madoff, Washington put more regulations in place, but that
still doesn't mean you don't have to keep an eye out for this type of
thing.

The Importance of Third-Party Custodians

Bernie Madoff was brought to court in 2008 and charged with
stealing about $50 billion dollars from his victims, who ranged from

private individuals to national banks. I am often asked how this could happen and how my investors are protected against this happening to them. I always reiterate to them that you need to know how to protect yourself. The reason Madoff was able to defraud investors over such a long period of time is glaringly apparent – he ran the show. He was his own custodian. What is a custodian? A custodian is defined as "a financial institution that holds customers' securities for safekeeping so as to minimize the risk of their theft or loss. A custodian holds securities and other assets in either electronic or physical form. Since the custodian is responsible for the safety of billions of dollars, they generally tend to be large reputable firms." Custodians have names like Schwab Advisor Services, TD Ameritrade Institutional, and Fidelity Institutional Wealth Services.

Acting as his own custodian, Madoff and his cohorts were able to create their own statements and submit them to investors with little or no scrutiny from a third party. You should ***always***, dear reader, make sure that a custodian bearing a different name than the advisory firm with whom you are doing business is between you and any money transaction. For instance, you may work with a Registered Investment Advisor with a name like "Global Worldwide Investment Services." That may be your money manager, but your assets are actually held at, say, Fidelity Institutional Wealth Services. This separation ensures that the advisor, who is making transactions on your behalf in your account, conducts those transactions only within your account. Assets are not allowed to leave the custodian without your personal approval. Some of the other benefits of a custodian are:

- o Reduced Opportunity: When your advisor uses a custodian, he or she will never directly touch your checks, deposits, or withdrawals. While your advisor can be given authority to make withdrawals, those withdrawals may only be directed to another account of yours, or sent by check to your address of record. If withdrawals are directed elsewhere, they will require your signature, and the custodian is responsible if funds leave your account due to a forged signature.

- o Advanced Technology for Signature Fraud: Custodians use advanced technology to detect signature fraud. The custodian will reject a signature and request verification if it fails authenticity checks performed by the custodian's signature matching technology. This detection process is very sophisticated and doesn't rely on the quick glance of a human eye to determine if the signature presented doesn't match previous signatures on file. In one case with which I'm familiar, a client of ours turned in a signature that was rejected by the custodian. As it turned out, our client had recently contracted Parkinson's Disease and had difficulty signing his name as he once did. The matter was cleared up, but the client was comforted to know that such measures were taken to protect his assets.

- o Insurance: Custodians carry large insurance policies – both liability insurance to protect against errors and omissions, in case unauthorized transactions occur, SIPC insurance for undirected transactions, and FDIC coverage for cash positions.

- o Duplicate Statements: While your advisor may send you a summary of investments from time to time, you should receive a summary of your investments directly from the firm where your assets are held. Madoff pulled off his scheme by generating his own statements and sending them out to clients. This went on for years before anyone seriously questioned the veracity of what was printed on the statements. Had a third-party custodian been involved, investors would have received two statements – one from their custodian, such as Fidelity, Pershing, or Schwab, and another from their investment advisor – Madoff. This would have added another layer of scrutiny that would have completely ruined Madoff's scheme.

Over the last several years the SEC has tightened up the rules on investment advisors who take custody of their clients' assets, but at the time of this writing, the SEC has yet to make it a requirement that such advisors use a third-party custodian. Investors should always exercise caution by comparing the statements received from the custodian with any correspondence received from the advisor. Even though stricter regulations are now in place, the door is still left open for fraud. Why would an investor want to do business with a firm that did not use third-party custodians? There are simply too many investment advisors to choose from who take the added precaution of using reputable third-party custodians; it makes little sense not to take advantage of that layer of safety.

Never Make the Check Out to the Advisor

Some of the most heart-wrenching cases of fraud I've witnessed came from situations where the investment advisor, or the insurance agent, told the clients to make their check out to them personally and they would "handle the funds" for them. A close friend and client experienced this first-hand prior to becoming a client of our firm. When I first met with them in 2012, I noticed they were skeptical and fearful of the investment world. They had all the reason in the world to feel that way. Several years prior to our first meeting, they met a well-known investment advisor who sold them on fixed guarantees of Canadian banks. They were coerced into signing over their life savings to this advisor. They wrote a series of checks to him after he explained to them that he would invest their funds in Canadian bank CDs. They even received receipts from reputable banks showing their funds were deposited. They later found that this advisor had been fabricating receipts and using client funds for his own benefit. You should NEVER make a check out to the advisor you will be working with, or to his or her firm. If an advisor requests this from you, please exercise caution.

Chapter Seven

Breaking Up With Your Financial Advisor Is Hard to Do

The most beautiful discovery true friends make is that they can grow separately without growing apart. ~ Elisabeth Foley

To borrow from the immortal lyrics of Neil Sedaka, "breaking up is hard to do." If you are at or nearing retirement, and you have an accumulation advisor whose dialogue no longer makes good investing sense to you, I'm sorry, but it's time to break up. I know, changing financial advisors can be one of the most awkward and difficult situations you will experience since you broke up with your high school sweetheart. It's a little uncomfortable at first, spurned lover syndrome and all of that. They may beg, offering to do anything to meet your needs and win you back. A good line to use is that you still "want to be friends," or "It's not you, it's me." It may be a difficult adjustment to make, sort of like a rock star changing barbers, but keep in mind, it's for the best. And once it's over, you can move on with your financial life and things will get better for you.

What's especially difficult is when you have been going steady with your financial advisor all through your working years. But look at it this way...you no longer see a pediatrician when you reach adulthood, and you don't consult your podiatrist for dental work. We understand perfectly well when it's time to change doctors through the different stages of life, or when we experience an issue with our health. It's much the same when dealing with wealth issues. Just as doctors have their own areas of expertise, so do financial advisors. Whether they deal in risk or safety is something you must determine for yourself.

What if your advisor is your best friend? Well, I have to admit… that is a tough one. It becomes a personal issue. You don't want to risk losing a good friend, but, on the other hand, you probably don't want to risk losing your money in retirement either. So it may come down to how much that friendship is worth in terms of dollars and cents. I do know some retirees who have allowed their portfolio to continue to underperform for years because they didn't want to hurt anyone's feelings. But I've known others who have come to the conclusion that if the friendship hinged on their continuing a business relationship that was no longer mutually beneficial, then it must have been a shallow friendship to begin with. In the end, it's a personal decision.

> "You just slip out the back, Jack
> Make a new plan, Stan
> You don't need to be coy, Roy
> Just get yourself free
> Hop on the bus, Gus
> You don't need to discuss much
> Just drop off the key, Lee
> And get yourself free"
>
> Paul Simon, American Singer/
> Songwriter
> Fifty Ways to Leave Your Lover

The transition from one advisor to another can be made with a simple phone call, an email, or letter. Other times, you may want to introduce your previous advisor to your new advisor. This can be more pleasant than you might think, because if your current advisor is truly a friend, then he or she may recognize his or her limitations when it comes to the handling your financial affairs. You may own a Lexus and may have developed a special relationship with the folks who run the service department at the Lexus dealership. But if you trade that Lexus in for a Mercedes, it is doubtful that your pals at the old dealership will view you with contempt if you now begin to take your automobile to the dealership that is fully certified and qualified to work on your car. Know when it is time to move on and recognize the importance of your financial future.

Chapter Eight

The Importance of Chemistry and Trust When Choosing an Advisor

It takes 20 years to build a reputation and five minutes to ruin it.

Warren Buffet

When it comes to choosing a financial advisor, trust is a fundamental criterion. Come to think about it, that's true with just about any business relationship, isn't it? If you don't trust your plumber, you're unlikely to let him work on your pipes. But trust is more important than ever these days – and rightly so. You must trust your advisor and your advisor must trust you.

We call the indefinable attraction that sometimes defines human relationships "chemistry." Chemistry of a different kind plays an important role in choosing a financial advisor. Do the advisor and the one being advised share the same investing philosophy? Are they on the same page? If they are, then the chemistry is good. Good chemistry is when both client and advisor speak the same financial language and their priorities match. In this regard, there are some things that only you can define, so you have to follow your instincts. You will know if your thinking aligns with your prospective financial advisor when, during the initial interview, the dialogue produced is in synchrony with your values and goals. If at any time during the interview process you feel that chemistry is simply not there, it would be in your best interests to politely excuse yourself, bid him or her goodbye, and keep on looking.

Close, but not too close ...

Your relationship with your advisor will be a professional one, true, but if you have some common interests, it will allow you to get to know each other on a higher level. This is more important to some people than others. I like to make myself available for this type of interaction if the client places a value on it. Nothing is more enjoyable than getting to know people over dinner or on the golf course if it seems mutually desirable. It's amazing to me how much I find I have in common with clients sometimes when we spend "off duty" time together. I have to say that my best client relationships are developed when I am able to assist them on a professional level and get to know them on a personal level, as well. That doesn't mean we become best friends, or BFFs, as the young people say, but the amicable relationship does help the gears of the financial planning process mesh more smoothly.

Having said the above, let me issue a word of caution on the subject. I've seen individuals who cannot seem to separate the business or professional aspects of the client-advisor relationship from the personal. This can be hazardous to your wealth. Working with an advisor because he or she is a relative or personal friend is, of course, acceptable. But if you don't share the same viewpoint and mindset with it comes to the handling of your money, it makes for bad Karma. Maybe you want to be kind to your nephew and help the young man get his start in the financial advisory business. That speaks well for your generous spirit and kind disposition. But once that personal relationship is coupled with the business layer, it can be difficult to dissolve. You need to maintain the prerogative to criticize and overrule your advisor if you feel he or she is not on the right track. Besides that, you must be able to dissolve the business relationship if you feel things aren't working to your advantage financially. If the personal relationship is too close, it may be difficult to pull off without injured feelings. You may get those "looks" at the next family reunion, and you don't want that.

Practice What You Preach

Some may feel that asking advisors personal questions about how they use their money is crossing a line. I disagree. How else will you know if your financial advisor believes in his or her own advice? If they recommend a particular concept as the best thing to sink your money into since sliced bread and vanilla ice cream, have they taken the plunge? It's a legitimate question. As an advisor, I believe full disclosure is important. Money questions are not personal. They are professional. It is our duty to invest our money the same way we invest our clients' money, if the investment is compatible with our personal financial goals. Age is obviously a factor in this. What may be good advice and acceptable for a younger advisor, for example, may not be appropriate for an older client. But all things being equal, there should still at least be similarities in the way your advisor is investing and the recommendations he or she gives you.

I once met a couple who stepped into my office for a first appointment. They said they thought it would be nice to see what was out there and explore a bit. After talking for 15 minutes or so, I discovered that he was a previous "financial advisor." The reason financial advisor is in quotation marks here is because he was, and admittedly so, a variable annuity salesman. He spent over 25 years of his life selling variable annuities. I asked the couple if they would allow me to look at their personal portfolio. He agreed, and guess what? Not one variable annuity! When we spoke later, he even told me he had never owned a variable annuity in his life. That blows me away. How could anyone ever sell any product, especially a financial product, that they didn't believe in? If your Culligan man uses a Kenmore water softener, would you not question his motives? Exercise caution and know what your potential advisor truly believes in.

Regular Reviews

How often should you meet with your advisor? This question is more complex than you might think. It depends on your level of financial knowledge, the type of plan that was put in place, and how long you have been with your advisor. Once a year is a bare minimum.

Knowledge: If you're financially savvy and you thoroughly understand all of the investments, and you understand how those investments should evolve over time, then maybe you are a once a year type of person. On the other hand, if you're unsure of exactly how your investments should work over time, then it may be more appropriate to meet with your advisor two, three, even four times per year.

Plan put in place: Without question, the more aggressive your investments are, the more often you should meet with your advisor. The market can move at a rapid pace sometimes. If you are in aggressive investments, then you need to be fully informed about the impact these moves have on your portfolio. On the other hand, if you are a very conservative investor and you are using "set-it-and-forget-it" investments, then there is no need to meet quite as often. If you have your assets placed in fixed annuities, for example, it may be appropriate to meet only once per year since the value of those accounts will change only once per year and there is usually very little to say in between contract anniversaries.

Time Heals All Wounds When you are working with a new financial advisor, it is wise to meet with them on a regular basis. I suggest quarterly meetings with a new advisor just to make sure you are in sync. Frequent meetings promote a greater understanding on the part of the client of how the financial plan is taking shape. The advisor is also able to ascertain if he or she is performing according to the client's wishes in all matters. As time passes, and you develop a greater understanding of the financial plan you have in place, and the advisor's business and investment philosophy, you will develop a higher level of comfort and knowledge. This is true even if your investments are on autopilot and your assets are conservatively placed, especially if the relationship is fewer than 24 months old. I like to offer all of my clients the opportunity to meet with me once per quarter and let them decide if it is to be less frequently. In most cases, quarterly meetings are sufficient unless we are working through a difficult problem.

The Three-Step Process I know there is such a thing as love at first sight. There may be occasions when couples fall in love on the first date and marry as soon as possible. In affairs of the heart, there may be some justification for making important decisions suddenly (although I don't recommend it), but not when it comes to your money. I don't think you can know who your advisor really is after the first meeting. Let's face it, someone courting your business may talk a good game, but there are key ways to ascertain who they truly are in the business sense of that expression before you decide to work with them. It's prudent to reserve judgment until you've done some due diligence in this regard. Take your time to go through this process. I recommend a three-step process.

The first meeting should give you the chance to determine if the advisors with whom you are meeting are the right fit for you. It gives the advisor an opportunity to determine the same. This should be an evaluation meeting, giving you an opportunity to get better acquainted. The advisor will be able to ascertain your goals and dreams, and you will be able to ascertain how the advisor thinks and what his planning philosophy is.

The second meeting should give you the chance to take things to the next level. The second meeting is what I refer to as a "strategy session." This is where you obtain a view from 20,000 feet up, so to speak, and come away with an analysis of your current situation that will allow you to start building a strategy to meet those concerns you have brought to the table. This should be a very interactive meeting, giving you the opportunity to better hone exactly what you are trying to achieve.

The third meeting should be the implementation meeting where you may begin to discuss the more specific details of your overall plan. This is an appropriate time to make a decision if you wish to proceed. Don't feel rushed. It may take five or six meetings. Take your time. Don't make a move until you are completely comfortable. The financial planning process is just that … a process.

Some financial advisors are too quick to pull out the solution – the next best mutual fund, the silver bullet annuity, or the next great evolution in life insurance. If you walked into a doctor's office and they started prescribing medication immediately without knowing all of your personal information, all the medications you are currently on, your physical activity, your living environment, your medical history, etc., would you feel comfortable? If you're looking for a quick fix for your allergies, or simple cold medicine, you can just go to the nearest local pharmacy. But if you're seeking a solution to a more in-depth medical problem or symptom, you will seek the help of a specialist and expect nothing less than a thorough examination. The same is true with financial advice and guidance. An effective strategy takes time and lots of analysis of your individual situation. Be wary of a quick fix. It should be a red flag when an advisor offers a solution in the first meeting.

Client Events

Many advisors hold regular client events in order to get clients involved and build a stronger bond with them. These can be anything from a dinner to a golf outing, but they can serve as a great opportunity for you to get a better idea of who your advisor is and if you fit in with the rest of the firm's clientele. It should be a red flag to you if the advisor you are considering does not hold these client dinners or outings. It may be a sign that some of the clients aren't exactly happy campers.

I must say that our client events are the most enjoyable affairs of the year for me, my staff members, and our clients. Our firm's first client event was held in the fall of 2008. If you remember the economic climate at that time, then you know that financial advisors as a group were not exactly occupying a top spot on the most popular people list. Some advisors whose practices were confined solely to market-based investments were running for cover and not answering their telephones. I doubt if many of them relished the idea of getting all of their clients together in one room, at least not without a bulletproof vest! Imagine if you would have had the opportunity to attend a potential advisor's client event in a year like 2008. But happily, our first client get-together was a most pleasant affair and none of our clients were angry or sad because their savings had been decimated by the sudden free-fall experienced by the stock market that year. Specializing in retirement planning and safe-money investments has its advantages.

We found this activity to be such a pleasant experience that we decided to hold client events every few months and invite prospective clients to attend and check us out. I'm not saying this to drum up business or toot my own horn, but if you can find an advisor that does this, it speaks volumes about who your advisor really is. Plus, you may have a great opportunity to forge a clear impression of whether the advisor with whom you are working is the right advisor for you.

References

If you're in business and you make a hiring decision, you will ask for references, and rightly so. You likely don't know the individual who is applying for the job, and you need to know them before you hire them. This will give you a clearer picture of their character, skills, and reliability. When evaluating an advisor, you may be surprised to find they don't always provide client references. This is because providing a client as a reference could violate SEC restrictions against the use of testimonials. Don't be discouraged if you come across this situation. The advisor is simply following rules and regulations. This is a good thing. You want your advisor to follow the rules, this illustrates character.

However, because of the difficulty in interpreting the law, many advisors will still furnish a couple of client references. In fact, I would highly recommend that you ask, but don't be discouraged if you are refused. How much weight you attach to the opinions about the prospective advisor will be, of course, up to you. Any advisor who has experienced any degree of success in his practice should have a substantial number of clients, and at least a handful of them should be willing to serve as references to his character, competency, and reliability. Has anyone ever asked you to provide personal or business references? Did you ever give the person requesting such references the names of anyone who you felt didn't like you, approve of you and the way you do business, or who was dissatisfied with your service? Of course not. So you may take that into consideration when you make the call to check on the references supplied to you by your prospective financial advisor. I think they call it, "taking with a grain of salt" the platitudes that may be offered by such ones. But that doesn't mean that this won't afford you an excellent opportunity to "listen between the lines," so to speak, and thereby make a better judgment as to how you would be treated as a client. It may be helpful to write down a few brief questions to keep your phone call with these references on track. Here are some questions that you may ask:

- What types of investments have been recommended to you?
- Have your investments been successful?
- Do you feel you are treated with respect?
- How often do you have contact with your advisor?
- Do you feel your questions are answered in a timely manner?
- Do you feel your advisor has covered all of your bases?
- Do they have what it takes?

Chapter Nine

Choosing a Professional

If you think a professional is expensive, wait 'til you try an amateur.
~Paul "Red" Adair

During the accumulation stage of life, when you're in your working years and you're building your nest egg, choices are easier and decisions you make on how to handle your finances aren't as critical as they will become later. As an earlier chapter that discussed dollar cost averaging showed, time is on your side. Even a volatile market cannot hurt you in the long run. (Disclaimer: Dollar Cost Averaging will not protect you from market losses.) But once you are nearing what I call the "red zone" of retirement, which is within 10 years on either side of retirement, the decisions you make are more difficult. More precision is needed by you and your advisor when you cross that line of demarcation between accumulation and distribution because more is at stake. In short, you want to make sure you're dealing with a true professional.

The dictionary defines a "professional" as a person who engages in an activity with great competence. Taken a step further, a true professional is one who attained the required knowledge, experience, and credentials necessary to take on the complex situations that will present themselves during your retirement years.

As you worked your way through the accumulation stages of life, you probably worked with an advisor who didn't hesitate to place your assets at risk in order to maximize their growth potential. That's a polite way of saying you probably allowed them to gamble with your money. Your advisor's mission was to "grow your wealth at all costs" to help you get to that glory land called retirement.

Believe it or not, it isn't that hard to invest for growth over long periods of time. Simply investing in the Standard and Poors (S&P) 500 or the Dow Jones Industrial Average (DJIA), and riding the market wave would have created some very solid returns. From December 30, 2003, to December 31, 2012, the S&P 500 returned 61.4%. From January 4, 1993, to January 2, 2013, the S&P 500 returned 222.61%. (Source: Google Finance) As you can see, you could have simply bought a handful of the largest stocks in the market and created substantial returns over a 10- or 20-year period. You wouldn't have even needed to understand what you were investing in!

Obviously it took a lot of hard work and sacrifice to build your wealth, but when it comes to investing in the market, a monkey could have thrown darts at the *Wall Street Journal* for big returns during those periods. As a matter of fact, such a theory was actually tested by the *Wall Street Journal* in 1988 after a well-known economist made the statement that "a blindfolded monkey throwing darts at a newspaper's financial pages could select a portfolio that would do just as well as one carefully selected by experts." Here's how the experiment went: The newspaper staff, standing in for the blindfolded monkeys, actually threw darts at a board on which were listed stock symbols. The other team consisted of investment experts who judiciously picked their own stocks to buy. Six months later the results of the two methods were revealed. After 100 such trials were conducted, the pros beat the "monkeys" 61-39, but the margin was slim enough for the professional investors to experience no small degree of embarrassment. What is even more astounding is that the pros barely beat the Dow Jones Industrial Average by a score of 51-49 in 100 matches. The actual returns were even more astounding. The professional investors netted an average return of 10.8% versus 4.5% for the dart throwers.

The announcement effect: Because the *Wall Street Journal* announced the professional's stock picks to their entire readership, it had the effect of artificially inflating the returns when the value of the selected stocks rose by copycat investors. Another factor to be considered is that the professionals picked riskier stocks. Professor

Bing Liang, who is an associate professor of finance and a faculty associate of the Center for International Securities and Derivatives Markets (CISDM) at Isenberg School of Management, University of Massachusetts-Amherst, says that, adjusted for risk, the pros would have lost 3.8% on the market over the six-month period.

What stands out most to me is the duration of the contest. It was quite brief. Had the "monkeys" had a little more time, perhaps they would have done even better. After the contest ended, the majority of "monkey" picked stocks continued to do well, while the stocks picked by the pros fell from their initial highs. And what about the fees? Obviously, if a professional were picking your stocks, you would have paid them. Incorporating fees would have further watered down the returns produced by these professional investors. While the *Wall Street Journal* never announced an ultimate winner, I think it can be inferred that the difference between what an investment professional can do over what you can do yourself during your accumulation years is marginal.

Once you get to retirement, your goals change drastically. You are no longer attempting to grow your wealth at all costs, but something much more difficult – preserving what you have and making it last a lifetime. Throw in the complicated facets of Social Security, Pension Optimization, Estate Planning, Inflation Protection, Health Insurance, Taxes, Long-Term Care risk, etc. and we can easily see how the job of your retirement planner is complex.

I once had an interview with a prospective client who explained to me how easy it was for him to accumulate the assets in his retirement account.

"I just told Human Resources how much money I wanted to defer into my 401(k) out of each paycheck, and it grew," he said. He went onto explain that once he got to retirement, however, he was like a lost puppy. Because he was the beneficiary of youth, time, and dollar cost averaging, saving wasn't difficult. The challenge lay in properly spending those assets so they would last him for the rest of his life.

"I learned that there is much greater complexity to that side of the financial picture," he said.

The Value of Experience

Financial advisors should not only have years of experience advising clients on their finances, but they should also have experience handling their own financial affairs as well. You should seek a professional who can prove that they "practice what they preach." Financial advisors who lack discipline and success in their own lives can hardly claim competency in directing the financial lives of others. There is nothing wrong with asking a potential advisor if they have taken the same precautions in their own financial lives that they're recommending to you. Ask them if they've ever been through bankruptcy or lost a significant amount through an investment. While some of the financial experiences I've had I would like to un-have, they all make for lessons learned. Overcoming obstacles and living through mistakes along the road to financial success can lead to a greater level of skill, and most certainly to a greater aptitude for mistake avoidance. Plainly, if your advisor can't create financial success in his or her own life, he or she probably can't perform that task for you.

Educational Requirements

Not much is required to hang out one's shingle as a financial advisor. The unfortunate truth is that many financial advisors lack the education, knowledge, credentials, and experience that is required to carry you through the ups and downs of your golden years. The bar for entry into the financial profession has been set quite low. Many firms don't even require a college degree. Many states, in fact, require no formal education or certification at all in order to set up shop as a financial advisor. However, there is typically a licensing exam required by the state to sell insurance or securities. These exams have varying degrees of difficulty and can usually be passed in a short period of time with minimal study. In contrast, however, some advisors put themselves through grueling, rigorous, and extensive educational programs to obtain such designations as Certified Financial Planner™ (CFP ©) and Chartered Financial Analyst (CFA). So, asking for an advisor's education and experience is fundamental in your search. I believe it should be one of the first questions you ask.

In addition, there are literally hundreds of designations and certifications with names that are deceptively impressive. Many advisors hold impressive-sounding credentials, some of which represent extraordinary achievements, but most do not. Before selecting your advisor, make sure you understand what his or her credentials really represent. For instance, a Certified Financial Planner™ now must have:

- Graduated with a bachelor's degree (or higher) from an accredited college or university.
- Successfully completed college-level course work encompassing financial planning, insurance planning, investment planning, income tax planning, retirement planning, estate planning, interpersonal communication, and the CFP © Board's Professional Conduct and Fiduciary Responsibility requirements. This coursework is equivalent to at least 18 credit hours, which can generally be completed in 18 to 24 months.
- Completed the Board's Financial Plan Development Course requiring presentation of a financial plan to the CFP © board.
- Completed a pass/fail 10-hour exam over a day and a half at a secure facility.
- Completed three years of full-time relevant personal financial planning experience, or two years of apprenticeship experience that meets additional requirements.
- Passed the CFP © board's Fitness Standards for Candidates and Registrants.
- Completed 30 hours of continuing education every two years.

In sharp contrast, the Certified Retirement Financial Advisor Certification Board only requires a four-day classroom course, no prior work experience, and no higher education; however, you do have to complete 15 hours of continuing education per year, which can be taken online by simply bypassing the class and taking a quiz. While this designation may sound very similar to a Certified

Financial Planner™, the two are in no way comparable. The financial services industry requires financial advisors to establish credibility with their clients. For this reason, an entire credentialing industry now exists to satisfy industry demand. Believe it or not, you could earn all of these credentials in less than 30 days – no prior work experience required!

- CAC – Certified Annuity Consultant – one-day class
- APP – Asset Protection Planner – 12-hour online or in person
- LTCIS – Long-Term Care Insurance Strategist – two-day class
- AIF – Accredited Investment Fiduciary – two and one-half day class
- CCPS – Certified College Planning Specialist – 18-25 hours self-study
- CWPP – Certified Wealth Preservation Planner – 24 hours online or in person
- CFG – Certified Financial Gerontologist – 24 hours self-study
- CSC – Certified Senior Consultant – 25 hours self-study
- CSA – Certified Senior Advisor – three and one half day "live" class
- AIFA – Accredited Investment Fiduciary Auditor – three and one half day class
- CDS – Certified Divorce Specialist – four-day workshop
- CRFA – Certified Retirement Financial Advisor – four-day class

How long have they been around?

The failure rate for legitimate financial advisors is incredibly high. It is one of the most difficult professions to succeed in, with the long hours and the high level of education required. According to Andre Cappon, president of the CBM Group, only 15% of advisors in training make it through their fourth year. That is why I recommend you find an advisor with a minimum of five years in practice. Many financial advisors have a high level of sales experience and are extremely charismatic, but personality can only take you so far. Sooner or later your performance will catch up to you.

Your Investment Team

When looking for your retirement advisor, recognize the value of a team approach. In retirement, your financial life becomes much more complicated. You will need to ensure that all of your bases are covered, mainly those of taxation, estate planning, and financial planning. Your retirement advisor should act as the quarterback of this team, assisting you with not only developing and implementing your plan, but bringing a team of experts to the table.

In the world of finance, we all have our areas of expertise. The Certified Public Accountant (CPA) has extensive experience in the area of accounting and tax. The attorney who specializes in estate planning will naturally have extensive experience in estate law. The Certified Financial Planner™ (CFP ©) should have general knowledge and experience in both of these areas *as well as* in the area of handling your investments, even though he or she specializes in the latter. You will most likely need all of these experts to work as a team, and your CFP © should act as quarterback or general contractor.

Why Advisor Continuity Is Important

It is important that your advisor have a contingency plan. The average age of a financial advisor today is 49, according to a 2010 report from Cerulli Associates, a Boston-based research firm. With an average retirement age of 64 for men and 62 for women, this would give the typical advisor only 13 to 15 more years in the workforce before he or she retires. How long do you plan to live in retirement? If you are a male and retire at age 64, your average life expectancy according to the Social Security Administration is around 82. This means you will be in retirement for approximately 18 years. What is deceptive about these actuarial life expectancy tables is that there is a 50% chance you will live past 82. How comfortable do you think you will be changing advisors, or worse, changing advisory firms when you are in your mid-80s? For this reason, it's important to find an advisor with a contingency plan. Your advisor should have a back-up plan in case of accident or retirement, preferably a younger advisor in training.

Fiduciary Standard

As you search for your retirement advisor, do you feel that this person should put your needs ahead of their own? Of course you do. But according to the Paladin Registry, those without a fiduciary duty to their clients outnumber fiduciary advisors 12 to one. Some industry estimates are even lower. So what is a fiduciary advisor, and how do you recognize the difference?

The statistics on this are quite revealing. There are approximately 800,000 financial advisors in America. However, based on licensing and registration data, 80% are not "real advisors, they are commission-based representatives. The remaining 20% that are "real advisors" hold one of two types of registrations. They are either Registered Investment Advisors (RIA) or Investment Advisor Representatives (IAR). An RIA refers to the registered entity and IAR refers to the actual registered person. These two registrations allow these advisors to provide advice and ongoing financial planning and asset management services for a fee. They are also fiduciaries, a legal obligation that holds them to the highest ethical standards in the financial services industry.

Fiduciaries are required by law and their own ethical standards to always place your needs ahead of their own. Isn't that a novel idea? It should be law, right? The other 80% of those who call themselves financial advisors are simply sales representatives who hold Series 6 or Series 7 securities licenses, which allow them to sell investment products for a commission. These sales reps are held to a much lower ethical standard called "suitability." Suitability at a very basic level means that what they are recommending is "okay" but not necessarily the best or lowest cost. The "suitable" recommendation may carry with it some of the highest fees in its category, but if it still performs the functions dictated by your needs, it may be deemed "suitable. The suitability standard still provides some legal protections for investors, but it isn't the gold standard. No, for that you need to ensure that your financial advisor is in fact an Investment Advisor Representative, Registered Investment Advisor, and/or Certified Financial Planner™™.

A serious legal battle is going on in Washington as I write this. Forbes issued an article on July 8, 2013, with the following comment:

> "Keep standards as simple as possible: Everyone who sells a financial product should be a fiduciary who puts investors' interests first. They should adhere to a time-honored legal definition that says they (advisers) can be held liable if they fail to protect their clients."

Bloomberg issued an article on March 1, 2013, with the following comment:

> "Authorized by the 2010 Dodd-Frank Act and advocated by a 2011 staff study, the SEC requested information today from the industry and public on costs and benefits of requiring brokers to give personalized investment advice that's in the best interest of clients. The current standard for brokers is lower, requiring that they sell products to clients that are suitable for them at the time of sale."

The trouble is that the titles of a true fiduciary advisor often overlap those of non-fiduciary advisors. The latter hold such titles as sales representative, investment representative, financial planner, insurance advisor, or financial consultant, but they are typically not bound by a fiduciary duty. For further explanation, I offer an example using the Merrill Lynch Growth Fund. Many large financial institutions manufacture their own investments, push them on their brokers, who then push them onto their clients. These are called "proprietary funds." Proprietary funds may carry higher fees and expenses in comparison to non-proprietary funds. Your broker can sell you this proprietary fund, because it is "okay," since it falls within suitability guidelines. Don't get me wrong. It's good to have suitability guidelines in place. Any advisor bound by suitability standards alone would be prevented from, say, convincing your grandmother to dump her entire life savings into Brazilian coffee bean futures. I don't know your grandmother, but she probably needs her retirement money to pay bills. Brazilian coffee beans may be a fine investment, but not for her.

On the other hand, a ***fiduciary*** is (a) required to hold client interest first, and (b) disclose any potential conflicts of interest that may exist. I am a fiduciary. If I were to recommend a growth mutual fund, for example, I would be required by law to determine ***which fund is the best*** for you by sifting through all the available growth funds. I would be required by law to explain why I chose one fund over another. Working with a fiduciary advisor safeguards you as to how you will be represented. In 2012, Mary Schapiro, SEC chairwoman stated, "I very much believe there should be a uniform standard of care" for registered Investment advisors and broker-dealers. The lack of uniform regulations for financial advisors has come to the forefront of government regulation. A fiduciary is defined, in law, as a person in a position of authority whom the law obligates to act solely on the behalf of the person he or she represents and in good faith. It should be an imperative that your advisor fit this definition.

Doing your homework

Is my advisor a convicted criminal? Believe it or not, convicted criminals can obtain a securities license, as long as their crimes occurred more than 10 years prior to application and weren't related to securities. Even as numerous complaints pile up, they are often allowed to continue to hold onto their license to practice. This is why it is important to do your research. A few of the most important places you can research your financial advisor professional's history are:

FINRA BrokerCheck® is a website where you can research brokers and brokerage firms. If your advisor carries a securities license, you'll find them here. You will be able to view the jurisdictions in which they can conduct securities transactions, previous registrations, and employment history. You may determine if there have been any suspensions and disclosure events, such as certain criminal charges and convictions, formal investigations, and disciplinary actions initiated by regulators, customer disputes, and arbitrations, and financial disclosures, such as bankruptcies and unpaid judgments or liens.

If your potential retirement advisor is a Certified Financial Planner™, you can find their registration on the **CFP © Board**

website. This will disclose any disciplinary history or bankruptcies in the last 10 years.

SEC IARD Public Disclosure Site is a website where you can do similar research on investment advisor representatives and investment adviser firms.

Better Business Bureau (BBB) – Your financial advisor's practice should be registered with the BBB. According to the BBB's published accreditation standards, in order to be a member in good standing, you must build trust, establish and maintain a positive track record in the marketplace, advertise honestly, be transparent, honor promises, be responsive, safeguard privacy, and embody integrity. You may also check with your local chamber of commerce for complaints against any business entity.

National Ethics Bureau (NEA) – The National Ethics Bureau is a membership organization requiring an adherence to their code of ethics.

NAIC – The NAIC or National Association of Insurance Commissioners can assist you in the verification of the insurance licenses that your financial advisor holds.

FINRA also has a valuable tool for understanding professional designations at the following website: apps.finra.org/datadirectory/ 1/ prodesignations.aspx

Getting Paid – Natural Conflicts of Interest

There is never anything wrong with asking advisors how they are compensated, and what was their incentive to choose one investment over another. In fact, it should be their duty, in my opinion, to explain this to you up front. One of the dirty secrets of the brokerage industry is something called, "Pay-to-Play," or as it is more kindly referred to, a "preferred family of companies." A brokerage firm may choose to push a certain family of mutual funds or insurance companies because they receive extra incentives or "kickbacks" from these companies. There is nothing illegal about this as long as it is "adequately" disclosed to customers. Edward Jones, one of the most recognized names in the brokerage industry, has been cited multiple times for these types of kickbacks. In 2007, Edward Jones agreed to pay $75 million to settle charges related to its 529 college savings plans and preferred mutual fund family program, as it did not adequately disclose its financial incentives to sell mutual funds from the preferred families of mutual funds. Furthermore, Edward Jones settled without admitting to or denying the charges. As part of the settlement, Edward Jones agreed to increase disclosures on its preferred mutual fund family program and their 529 savings plan. You can view these disclosures now at www.edwardjones.com/groups/ejw_content/@ejw/documents/web_content/dweb244757.pdf. If you pull out your statement, you will be able to locate the link to this site. You be the judge as to how adequately this is disclosed.

In addition, why do you suppose you are generally offered two or three different options when it comes to annuities and life insurance with large brokerage firms? In general, large brokerage firms will limit the availability of products to their advisors in order to push a larger amount of business to their preferred carriers for, you guessed it, more kickbacks. While any additional compensation on mutual fund and variable annuity products is required to be disclosed, good luck finding the disclosure on your own.

These inherent conflicts of interest can be avoided by working with an independent financial advisory firm. An independent firm has the ability to shop the entire insurance, mutual fund, and securities markets for the best products to fit your needs. While there is still the potential for an advisor to receive additional incentive for choosing one product over another, at least they have the ability to shop around. And if you're working with a fiduciary advisor, they are required by law to offer you the best product for your given situation, regardless of compensation. They must also thoroughly explain to you the reasons for their recommendations.

Allow me to share with you an experience in this regard. I was working with a prospective client who was doing some shopping between financial advisors. This retiree needed a certain level of guaranteed income, so we shopped around and decided to use an A-rated carrier that would provide the highest level of income among all the other carriers. This client visited with another advisor who worked at a large brokerage firm. The client explained to the advisor what our firm recommended, including what insurance company we recommended. The prospective client returned to my office, quite disturbed by what he found. The competing advisor told him that his company wouldn't even allow him to sell that particular company's products because they were, in his words "bad."

After doing some research, (the research entailed visiting the broker's website and viewing the disclosure list of available products and kickbacks) we found the company this advisor worked for received kickbacks from half a dozen insurance companies, so they (presumably) would receive the lion's share of that brokerage firm's business. The product we recommended wasn't "bad" at all. In fact, it was actually a much stronger company financially and provided a higher level of income than the competing product that was recommended by the advisor at the large brokerage company. The point is, never just take an advisor's word for anything as being unmitigated gospel, regardless of the advisor's perceived trustworthiness or whatever charisma he or she may possess. Do your own research. Make your decisions accordingly.

What Is a "Fee Only" Advisor?

Many advisors operate on the basis of "fee only." In my opinion, this is the only way you should have your money managed in the market. I once had a cynical relative insist that I was happy about the 2008 market crash. He insinuated, in fact, that I had probably profited from it, as it gave me good reason to make changes within my clients' portfolios and profit by the transactions. It saddened me to think that this is the way many clients probably view their financial advisors. This is yet another reason why Wall Street, in my opinion, is broken.

If your advisor only makes money when changes are made to your portfolio, then what incentive do they have to make you more money other than merely to keep you as a client? I want my advisor to make changes to my portfolio as new opportunities arise, but solely for the purpose of increasing my returns or protecting me from loss. In contrast to a commissioned advisor, a fee - only advisor may make a certain percentage of assets under management annually. This means that if your portfolio grows, so does their income. Now your goals can be aligned. An advisor who is truly operating on a fee-only basis is often driven away from certain products that are necessary for your retirement. Things such as life insurance, long-term care insurance, and annuities. In order for your advisor to receive compensation for selling these products it must come in the form of a commission, or they simply don't get paid. Important aspects of your financial plan can be left out if you choose to work with a fee-only advisor. On the investment side of your portfolio, however, you should always work with a fee-based investment advisor.

Chapter Ten

Letting Purpose Drive Your Financial Life

Humility is not thinking less of yourself; it is thinking of yourself less. Humility is thinking more of others. Humble people are so focused on serving others, they don't think of themselves.

~ Rick Warren, The Purpose Driven Life:
What on Earth am I Here for?

Unless you give it a purpose, money is no more than numbers on a piece of paper. One of my first "paycheck" jobs was carrying golf bags at the local country club. I loved it. During summers, I was up like a shot at 4:30 every morning and at the golf course before 5 a.m., eager to assist customers. I got to know many people, some of them very wealthy. Walking the course with them, I got to know some of them quite well. I didn't just know them by name, I knew them as individuals. I knew what they liked, what they didn't like, and what made them tick. Even though I was a young lad, I viewed each of them as a friend, and I think they thought of me that way as well. In casual conversation they would sometimes leave me with golden nuggets of wisdom I could never have learned elsewhere. It was my observation that some of the kindest people I encountered were also the richest. Most of them had worked hard and been diligent about saving their money. If they were in business, they had an almost paternal caring spirit about them for their customers and their employees. I also concluded that the ones who seemed the happiest were not focused on themselves; they served others.

Later in life, I read books promoting the philosophy that making service to others your first priority, means success will follow just as surely as summer follows spring.

So it's not about the money. It's about what you want the money to do. When you're young, it's relatively simple to crystallize what you want money to do. You want it to buy those new shoes, that new dress, pay for hanging out with your peers. When you start out your adult life, you identify money with only what goods and services it will purchase. It will buy a home, a car, maybe a vacation with the family. It's only when you get older and begin accumulating some wealth that you should begin to crystallize what your ultimate purpose is for that wealth.

There is nothing difficult about setting goals. It's a matter of deciding what you want and writing it down. Deciding what you **really** want, however, may not be so easy. That may require some soul-searching. Finding the **why** is often so much more challenging than finding the how.

When I first began my adult life and entered the professional world, I was blessed with a treasure that few people my age possessed – a family tradition passed down from my grandfathers and two strong parents of putting others' needs ahead of my own. It wasn't a technique for doing business but a philosophical pathway of life. Assisting people with their financial problems came as natural to me as hefting those golf bags when I was a suntanned teenager on the country club links. Find the **real** problem and then go about looking for the best solution.

Early on in my career, I had a couple come into my office with a grocery bag full of account statements. The husband was retired and the wife, who also worked, was very close to retirement, but they were not at all at peace with this new phase of their lives. For one thing, they had so many small accounts of every kind that they didn't know where their money was, let alone how much it was earning in the way of interest, or what their losses were. He had been a contractor during his working years, and she was a nurse. They weren't detail-oriented when it came to their personal finances. Some of the statements in the grocery bags had never been opened.

I knew our first order of business was to help them sort out what they had and where they had it and why. That accomplished, we next set about helping the pair establish their goals. But to do that, we had to create specific purposes for their different investable assets. We created a metal box with hanging files and labeled file folders assigned to each specific purpose they identified. Now they could see each asset as a facilitator of one of their goals, not as an abstract with no assignment. They were able to "see" the account and interpret its features, such as liquidity, income, growth, and estate planning.

In the process, we were able to determine that the couple had more than they thought in the way of assets they could dedicate to income in retirement. Now her plans to retire could be solidified with peace of mind. They had a purpose-driven plan for the future with which they were comfortable.

"I feel like a great weight has been lifted from my shoulders," the woman said.

Experiences like that remind me of why it is that I do what I do. I need no more evidence than the smiles of relief on the faces of those I have been privileged to assist with their financial goals to convince me of why I am here and that my business philosophy of purpose-based planning was well chosen. Helping people find their financial purpose and providing them with the tools to accomplish that purpose is its own reward.

About the Author

Casey B. Weade, CFP ©, a leading retirement planning professional, is a sought-after speaker on progressive personal finance and retirement planning strategies. His "safer money" approach to investing, coupled with his track record of success, has made him a prominent authority on television, radio and many publications. As the president of Howard Bailey Financial, Inc., he works to provide comprehensive financial planning strategies to pre-retired and retired individuals,  helping them achieve total wealth optimization and reliable income sources in retirement. A firm believer in achieving success through a personalized strategy, Mr. Weade acts as each individual's financial coach working to optimize their current financial situations by managing and inimizing financial risks, tax liabilities and positioning accounts for continued growth–regardless of market volatility.

Mr. Weade graduated from Stetson University with a Bachelor's degree in Finance as a member of the honorary finance fraternity Beta Alpha Psi. He then went on to earn the prestigious Certified Financial Planner™ (CFP ©) certification through Kaplan University. He is also an Investment Advisor Representative (IAR) permitting him to advise on a variety of investments, as well as life, accident, and health insurance licensed and Long-Term Care Certified.

To go along with these credentials, Casey is also an approved member of the Extended Fiduciary Network™ (EFN), National Ethics Bureau™ (NEA) and the Better Business Bureau® (BBB), and the Financial Planning Association (FPA).